This book is dedicate
system w

LEGAL RIGHTS OF PRISONERS

Cases and Comments

James F. Anderson
and
Laronistine Dyson

University Press of America,® Inc.
Lanham · New York · Oxford

Co
Universit

Lanl

1
Cumnc

Printed in t
British Library Catalogi

Library of Congre

A
Legal rights of p
James F. And

1. Prisoners—Legal sta
2. Correctional law—Uni

ISBN 0-761
ISBN 0-761

The paper usec
requirements of Ame
Sciences—Permanen

TABLE OF CONTENTS

FOREWORD

The Eighth Amendment to the Constitution prohibits the infliction of "cruel and unusual punishments," but what is the meaning of "cruel"? What is the meaning of "unusual"? Courts, until recently, paid little attention to these questions, or to prisons in general. They followed what was known as the "hands-off" doctrine, deferring to the authority of corrections administrators and abdicating their responsibility to ensure that the rule of law is followed everywhere, including prisons. Prisoners were seen as little more than "slaves of the state," as one infamous court decision declared (*Ruffin v. Commonwealth*, 1871).

Beginning in the 1960s, federal courts began to more closely examine the conditions of confinement. Inmates began to file a number of lawsuits alleging constitutional deprivations from the mundane (being served the wrong type of peanut butter) to the serious (being assaulted by correctional officers). Judicial intervention became the norm rather than the exception in many state corrections departments, as district court judges discovered that the "hands-off" doctrine had allowed corrections administrators to largely ignore the rights of prisoners.

Prisoners won a number of cases in the 1970s. In particular, they were successful in gaining some due process rights under the Fourteenth Amendment and some limited First Amendment rights of speech and religion. Recently, however, the United States Supreme Court has refused to further extend the rights of prisoners, and the United States Congress has reacted to what it saw as unwarranted judicial activism on behalf of the undeserving by passing legislation restricting the ability of prisoners to file lawsuits. Currently, the prisoners' rights movement is at a standstill, or some might argue, moving backwards.

One may be tempted to say, so what if prisoners' claims are not received warmly by the courts? After all, prisoners are in prison because they have broken the law and been found guilty by a jury of their peers. Why shouldn't prisoners suffer? Why is the law of corrections worth our study? I would argue that how we treat our prisoners says something about us as a society and a democracy. We live by the rule of law. The outer limits of correctional practice are thus appropriately controlled by the law, particularly the Constitution.

James F. Anderson and Laronistine Dyson have written a book, which is intended to fill a significant gap in the typical criminal justice curriculum. The majority of introductory criminal justice textbooks give scant attention to the legal issues surrounding corrections, and relatively few criminal justice programs offer a course on the legal rights of inmates. Legal Rights of Prisoners: Cases and Comments is intended to serve as an introduction to this important, but understudied, aspect of the criminal justice system. It can serve as a supplemental reader or stand alone as the primary text for a class in corrections law. It is clearly written, and avoids the use of legal jargon.

The authors first provide the reader with an account of the development of the law in corrections, from the "hands-off" era to the prisoners' rights movement, and the period of judicial intervention to the current period of retrenchment. The authors then discuss the varieties of lawsuits and legal actions, which may be brought by inmates. Next, the authors discuss the various constitutional rights possessed by incarcerated offenders, including the First, Fourth, Eighth, and Fourteenth Amendments. The emphasis is on the case law, and readers are provided with well-edited excerpts of significant Supreme Court and lower court decisions regarding inmates' rights. The authors also include pedagogical aids, such as a list of key terms and a glossary. These are particularly useful to the undergraduate criminal justice student who may not have received prior exposure to the esoteric language of the law.

Prisons are sometimes seen as the end of the line, as places to dump those who cannot abide by society's rules. Even in such dank, dark places, however, the law is paramount. And even those who have broken the law are entitled to its protections. Corrections law shines a light on American society, and demonstrates the degree of compassion and the commitment that we possess to the rule of law. Protection of the rights of incarcerated individuals sends a message to all members of our society. The study of the law of prisoners' rights is an important, but sadly overlooked, aspect of the criminal justice curriculum. Legal Rights of Prisoners: Cases and Comments is a fine effort at remedying this unfortunate circumstance.

Craig Hemmens, J.D., Ph.D.
Department of Criminal Justice Administration
Boise State University
Boise, Idaho 83725

PREFACE

Legal Rights of Prisoners: Cases and Comments is unlike any other book written on case law of prisoners' rights. Whereas, other books simply list and provide a summary of cases that may, or may not, be directly related to prisoners' rights, this book provides separate chapters that address prisoners' rights protected by the First, Fourth, Eighth, and Fourteenth Amendments. These chapters provide a discussion of the meaning of each amendment and offer a list of pertinent cases decided over the past three decades by the federal court system. We selected these amendments because inmates use them to bring various claims against correctional facilities. They also show how decisions made by the U.S. Supreme, circuit, and district courts have affected the freedoms and restrictions placed upon prisoners.

This book begins with an introduction to American law. The reader is presented with the role and purpose of law in today's society. We then provide a comprehensive description of the corrections component of criminal justice. The characteristics of state and federal courts are used to provide the reader with a foundation of the structure of the American court system. Aspects of the civil rights movement of the 1960s are used to reveal how the prisoners' rights struggle was born and how offenders won the right to have their constitutional protections recognized in places of confinement. As time progressed, judicial activism affected the way correctional administrators and staff operated their prisons. In essence, correctional administrators, wardens, and guards were forced to operate their facilities in a manner consistent with constitutional safeguards and protection. As such, correctional officials saw their authority decline.

Prior to the 1960s, the courts (state and federal) chose not to get involved in cases where the plaintiff was an inmate. Since many of these cases were related to the conditions of confinement, the courts felt correctional administrators and staff were better able to make decisions which were related directly to these complaints. The types of cases, which then led to the courts becoming more involved in prisoner's rights litigation, are discussed in detail. We discuss the types of legal remedies inmates had prior to the movement, and now have today, to access the courts. These remedies include tort suits, the Civil Rights Act or Section 1983, the State Constitutional Rights Act, Habeas Corpus, and the Civil Rights of Institutionalized Persons Act. A smooth, but necessary transition, is made from legal remedies to the extensiveness of cases being filed by inmates today, along with an in-depth discussion of the high cost of inmate litigation.

Cases pertaining to each of the four amendments (First, Fourth, Eighth, and Fourteenth) are discussed in chronological order. Chapter Six explains which of the constitutional safeguards and protections under the First Amendment prisoners retain. Interpretation of the Fourth Amendment and what it means to prisoners' right to privacy are discussed in Chapter Seven. Excessive and deadly force, denial of protection and medical treatment, and other claims brought under the Eighth Amendment are provided in Chapter Eight. Chapter Nine addresses due process and equal protection rights that state inmates are entitled under the Fourteenth Amendment.

Before the prisoners' rights movement, the courts had long chosen to remain distant from litigation in which an inmate was the plaintiff. Since the movement began, the courts began their increasing involvement in these types of cases. Today, complaints by inmates have become excessive and have inundated the courts. Chapter Ten focuses on the Prison Litigation Reform Act of 1995, which places restrictions on an inmate's ability to file civil rights claims. The possibility of the courts again returning to a hands-off approach is explained. For example, since cases filed by inmates are flooding the courts, the justices may now decide to decrease their involvement in hearing these cases.

The cases that are summarized in this book were taken from several legal sources. This work is a compilation of federal cases that were decided in district, circuit, and the U.S. Supreme Courts. del Carmen contends that because of the esoteric nature of legal research, many readers are unfamiliar with legal citations. Therefore, we provide guidance to those citations that were decided by the Supreme Court since its decisions are binding on all courts in America.

U.S. United States Reports. This is the official source of the U.S. Supreme Court decisions. It is published by the United States Government.

S.Ct. Supreme Court Reporter. This reports U.S. Supreme Court cases and is published by the West Publishing Company, a private publisher.

Cr.L. Criminal Law Reporter. This reports U.S. Supreme Court decisions, and is published by the Bureau of National Affairs, Inc., a private publisher.

L.W. United States Law Week. This reports U.S. Supreme Court decisions, and it published by the Bureau of National Affairs, Inc.

One case that appears in this text is *Bell v. Wolfish*, 441 U.S. 520 (1979). This means that the case can be found in Volume 441 of the

United States Reports, starting on page 520 and was decided in 1979. Any case decided by the Supreme Court can have different citations and be found in different volumes and pages in the other sources listed above.

Though the target audience is the undergraduate student, this book may be used by graduate level and law students or anyone interested in learning more about the courts' involvement in inmate litigation. Since cases filed by inmates are being decided everyday, the reader should take into consideration that the interpretations provided in this book only cover the past three decades. At any moment, the courts could decide to take a different approach to inmate litigation, thus forever making another significant impact on the way in which inmates file suits against fellow inmates or others (administrators, wardens, guards, etc.) within the correctional system. The systematic approach used to describe the cases, as they relate to each amendment, was critical in determining past, present, and future movements (decisions made) by the courts. This approach, combined with an ever-changing court and criminal justice system, has allowed us to present the plight of prisoners' rights in the most objective manner possible.

ACKNOWLEDGMENTS

A project of this magnitude can never be successfully completed without the help of many people providing guidance, support, constructive criticism, and inspiration. As such, the authors of this book would like to express sincere appreciation to everyone involved in its completion.

The first author of this work wishes to express appreciation to colleagues in the Department of Sociology, Criminal Justice, and Criminology at the University of Missouri-Kansas City for their unending support and encouragement. Special thanks is given to professors Jerald C. Burns and Karen Taylor at Alabama State University and Willie Brooks Jr., at The Victoria College for spending countless hours reading and providing invaluable suggestions on how to improve the quality of the manuscript. I would like to express appreciation to Dr. Bankole Thompson at Eastern Kentucky University and to professors Tazinski Lee at Mississippi Valley State University and David Spinner at the University of Maryland-Eastern Shore. Special thanks is also given to Dr. Francis P. Reddington at Central Missouri State University and to Dr. Adam Langsam at the University of North Texas. Finally, the first author wishes to express gratitude to three former graduate students (Daryl Kosiak, Gary Kowaluk, Elizabeth K. Springate) of Corrections and the Constitution for inspiring this work.

The second author would like to thank those who provided continuous encouragement throughout this project: All of her students at Kentucky State University who questioned her about her writing projects each time they visited her office and tried to get copies of the book long before it was released; Pamela Young of North Carolina A&T University and Kenneth and Jean Clay, for the never-ending prayers, especially when things got really rough; and big brothers, First Sergeants M.D. Nicholson and J.T. Royster, for always saying the right words I needed to hear to squeeze even more hours from the day to work on my writing. You have truly been a blessing to me.

The authors would especially like to thank Dr. Andres Rodriquez and Robyn Anderson-Terhort for providing copy editing, proofreading, and technical support.

INTRODUCTION

In the 1960s, prisons were places where many wardens and penal administrators managed their institutions with absolute power and control. Some scholars contend that maintaining order, not **rehabilitation** or treatment, was the primary concern for many administrators. In order to effectively manage an inmate population, wardens accepted an autocratic model, arguing that without strong administrative control, riots, disorder, and violence would become pervasive in correctional facilities affecting prison officials, as well as prisoners. Therefore, correctional administrators exerted power and control over every aspect of the institutions they managed. Others concurred in the belief that correctional managerial control deterred violence in penal settings. The old adage "absolute power corrupts absolutely" proved to be true in many correctional institutions before the reform era. Since prisoners literally had no voice to represent their interests, they served their sentences at the pleasure of the administrator. During this time, it was not uncommon for inmates to endure insufferable conditions, such as violence, denial of baths and adequate medical care, improper ventilation, denial of religious freedom, denial of visitation, and long hours of forced labor at correctional facilities. Moreover, at the same time, many inmates were leased to companies, for a wage that competed in the open market with other companies, to build and manufacture products. These inmates were exploited as cheap labor. They worked extensive hours each day and were typically treated inhumanely by being denied adequate food, clothing, equipment, and medical care when needed. Consequently, some were shot to death while trying to escape brutal working conditions.

Prior to the 60s, correctional managers enjoyed a free reign on running penal facilities the way they saw fit, since there was very little outside intervention from the courts or the free society with respect to the operations of places of confinement. However, this situation would drastically change as the courts began entertaining inmates' (Black Muslims) complaints that voiced concerns over religious freedom and the operations of prisons during the turbulent sixties, with its many revolutions for racial and social justice in all areas of American life.

As the 60s progressed into the 70s, the federal courts put to rest its hands-off approach on correctional matters to the point where it was criticized for being too receptive in landscaping correctional law, or the struggle for prisoners' rights. Critics charged that many correctional administrators, wardens, and guards saw their authority decline as **judicial activism** began to affect prison systems. With diminished power, prison officials witnessed growing problems in their institutions that came with prisoners' newly recognized rights. Some of the problems included an abundance of frivolous lawsuits filed, riots, gangs, drugs, fights, random violence, rapes, disrespect of administrative orders, and lawlessness. Advocates of the **prisoners' rights movement**, on the other hand, argue that prisons are better places today because of the sweeping reforms that were made in the past several decades. They also contend that prisons are more humane now than ever before in the nation's history. Despite this claim, what rights do prisoners enjoy? Have they been expanded even more since the advent of the prisoners' rights revolution of 1960s? Or has the Supreme Court started a quiet revolution to revert to a hands-off approach? This book provides important case history, including some of the more recent cases, that the federal courts and Supreme Court have decided on the constitutional rights of inmates, and signals the direction in which the courts are headed with respect to the rights of those in places of confinement.

Legal Rights of Prisoners: Cases and Comments contains eleven chapters. Chapter One, entitled "An Introduction to American Law," introduces the student to the role and purpose of law in contemporary society. More specifically, this chapter addresses the historical origins of the law and outlines a discussion of the court system in present day American society. It also delineates between state and federal courts, and provides the student with a dialogue on the foundation of **criminal law**, as well as **civil law**.

Chapter Two, entitled "The Corrections Component of Criminal Justice," argues that because there are so many offenders in the corrections system, alternatives to traditional incarceration programs have been created to accommodate offenders and to give nonviolent offenders a reprieve from **secure confinement**. As such, the chapter provides a number of intermediate sanction programs to which offenders could be sentenced, depending on the seriousness of their law violations. Moreover, the chapter discusses the process of justice. The student is introduced to the administration of justice and the other components that compose the criminal justice system -- police and courts. This chapter offers the student a systemic perspective on how corrections fit within the overall scheme of the administration of justice.

Chapter Three, "From Hands-off to Hands-on," presents the emergence of the prison rights movement that started in the 1960s. The chapter discusses many of the events (social and political) that ultimately led to the federal court system entertaining the complaints and challenges of constitutional violations of prisoners.

Chapter Four, "Types of Lawsuits and Petitions Brought by Inmates," argues that inmates today are not subjected to the whim of their captors, as were inmates prior to the prisoners' rights movement of the 1960s, but rather, they have mechanisms to voice complaints and even challenge conditions of their confinement. The chapter introduces and provides a detailed discussion of legal remedies to access the courts and petition the government for a redress of grievances. These remedies include tort suits, the **Civil Rights Act** or **Section 1983**, the **State Constitutional Rights Act**, Habeas Corpus, and the **Civil Rights of Institutionalized Persons Act**.

In Chapter Five, "Preventing Inmate Litigation," a discussion is provided that explains how pervasive and expensive inmate litigation is and what penal administrators can do to safeguard against being sued. The chapter offers information on the consequences of a lawsuit if a **special master** is appointed by the court to oversee compliance with a **consent decree**. The chapter also gives strategies that administrators can use to protect themselves from successful inmate litigation, and some defenses that administrators use to justify the regulations and practices that occur in their facilities.

Chapter Six is entitled "Inmates and the **First Amendment**." This chapter defines what is contained in the First Amendment and explains which constitutional safeguards and protections prisoners retain. Moreover, it lists issues that inmates bring under the First Amendment, such as freedom to receive and send mail, freedom of the press, freedom of religion, access to court, and the right to association and visitation. It also provides a host of cases that were decided by federal courts, as well as the Supreme Court, on these issues.

Chapter Seven is entitled "Inmates and the **Fourth Amendment**." The chapter provides a discussion and interpretation of what the Fourth Amendment means to prisoners within the context of their confinement. It addresses whether or not prisoners have a right to privacy and can be free from institutional searches of all types, ranging from a pat-down or cell search to a **body cavity search**. This chapter provides pertinent cases that have addressed the Fourth Amendment challenges of prisoners.

Chapter Eight, titled, "Inmates and the **Eighth Amendment**," provides a definition and interpretation of the amendment. It presents a discussion of excessive and deadly force, denial of protection, denial of medical treatment, and other claims that inmates bring under the amendment. In addition, the chapter includes cases that the federal tribunals and Supreme Court have decided concerning the issue of cruel and unusual punishment.

Chapter Nine, entitled "Inmates and the **Fourteenth Amendment**," provides the reader with a definition and interpretation of the due process and **equal protection** clauses found in this amendment. It discusses how the amendment is binding on state governments. This chapter specifically addresses the due process to which inmates are entitled in cases where they face disciplinary proceedings, transfers, reclassification, the loss of good time credits, and punitive segregation, to name only a few.

Chapter Ten, "Reverting to a Hands-off Approach," argues that the federal courts are not as receptive towards inmate litigation as they were during the prison rights movement. This chapter argues that the federal courts, including the Supreme Court and congressional legislation, are making it increasingly difficult for inmates to have claims heard in court. The chapter focuses on the **Prison Litigation Reform Act of 1995** (which places restrictions on inmates' ability to file Section 1983 litigations), the Cases decline of issuing the Writ of Habeas Corpus, and the impact of *Turner v. Safley* (which is arguably one of the most important cases in correctional law). This chapter argues that these three mechanisms appear to signal the courts reverting to a hands-off approach and moving away from judicial activism.

Chapter Eleven, "The Future of Inmates' Rights and Litigations," offers predictions on the direction that correctional law will continue to take in the future. It also addresses some new areas where litigation might be focused. In the final analysis, Legal Rights of Prisoners: Cases and Comments offers a complete discussion of the legal rights of prisoners and the claims that inmates typically bring before the court for redress.

CHAPTER 1

An Introduction to American Law

FOCAL POINTS

- Introduction to American Law
- Historical Origins of the Law
- A Dual Court System
- Getting to the Supreme Court
- The Foundations of the Criminal Law
- Key Terms

America is a nation of laws. All facets of the American experience are regulated by laws. Indeed, the **Bill of Rights** (see Appendix), U.S. Constitution, and state constitutions comprise the bedrock of American life. The Fourteenth Amendment is incorporated into some of the Bill of Rights to make the amendments applicable to the state, as well as the federal government. The **Supreme Court** has not quite gone so far as to incorporate into the Fourteenth Amendment all the applicable provisions of the Bill of Rights, but it has come very close to doing so. The Court applies the doctrine of **selective incorporation**, which is also known as **selective absorption**. According to this view, the Fourteenth Amendment's due process clause does not prescribe any specific procedure for the administration of justice or the execution of governmental affairs. Instead, it forbids states to adopt a procedure that "offends some principle of justice so rooted in the traditions and consciousness of our people as to be ranked fundamental" or to deprive people of rights "implicit in the concept of ordered liberty." The application of this general standard of fundamental fairness has resulted in the selective incorporation into the due process clause of almost all the provisions of the Bill of Rights. Those few not incorporated merely provide certain procedures that will secure justice, but they are not the only procedures that will do so. By 1970, the Bill of Rights had been incorporated into the Fourteenth Amendment. Today, except for the Second, Third, and Tenth Amendments, which are not applicable, the Fourteenth Amendment imposes on states all the requirements that the Bill of Rights imposes on the national government.

The Role of Law in Society

Law is defined as the body of rules of specific conduct prescribed by an existing legitimate authority in a particular jurisdiction and at a particular point in time (Grilliot, 1983). The law defines those behaviors that are labeled criminal. It describes the procedures to be followed under our adversarial system by those with the responsibility of law enforcement, adjudication, and corrections (Cripe, 1997).

Law is a dynamic force for maintaining social order and preventing chaos in society (Spiro and Houghteling, 1981; Goldman and Jahnige, 1985; Corwin and Peltason, 1988). It is difficult to imagine the existence of a society or community without laws regulating behavior. The law embodies the story of a nation's development through the centuries. From primitive customs, codes, and practices, the law of our nation has evolved into a sophisticated system administered by highly trained jurists (Abraham, 1987; Wasby, 1989). The present legal system in the United States represents years of struggle and thought. Law is a dynamic process by which rules are constantly being adopted and changed to keep pace with the complexities of an evolving society.

A community of people uses legal constitutions to create and administer law (Cripe, 1997). In the United States, the legislative, executive, and judicial branches, and the administrative agencies of the federal and local governments perform the law-making and administrative functions. The law is divided into the following categories: Constitutional law, case law, statute law, treaties, executive orders, regulations of administrative agencies, and local ordinances.

The United States Constitution is the supreme law of the land (Spiro and Houghteling,1981; Goldman and Jahnige, 1985; and Corwin and Peltason, 1988). Any state constitutional provision or federal, state, or local law that is repugnant to the Constitution is rendered invalid. However, the law is not merely a technical institution used for economic or political purposes; its function has greater importance (Cripe, 1997). Because moral and legal questions overlap in a democratic society, the law tends to mirror the people's basic values.

Historical Origins of the Law

American law was influenced by several early written legal codes that include the Code of Hammurabi, Mosaic Law, and Rome's Twelve Tables. However, the greatest influence on American law has been England's common law tradition. The **common law** essentially refers to law common to all subjects of the land without regard for geographical or social differences. It was judge-made law, or case law, because crimes were defined and created by judges. It was a constantly evolving legal code (Grillot, 1983). Some scholars argue that common law came into being with the Norman Conquest of 1066 by William the Conqueror under the reign of Henry II. After the conquest, the church handled sinful acts, the royal administration handled the most serious crimes, and *stare decisis* (let the previous decision stand) emerged whereby royal judges used previous cases to render decisions on present cases. This eventually fostered consistency in the application of law (Grillot, 1983). Cripe (1997) contends that common law was used in the American colonies before the revolution. However, after the revolution, the colonies did not adopt the law in its totality, but rather changed the law to fit their needs. For example, if a certain law was viewed as inadequate, colonies would create **statutes** to address their concerns.

Courts

Courts are places where legal disputes are settled. They can either have original or appellate **jurisdiction**. Original jurisdiction is the authority of the court to hear or try a case. This is based on geography and the subject matter in question. Appellate jurisdiction is the authority of a court to review a decision made by a lower court. Venue is place oriented. It flows from the policy of the law to have cases tried in the place where the crime was committed, i.e. where a party resides, or where another consideration makes trial in that area justifiable (Grilliot, 1983). The motion for a **change of venue** is usually filed by the defendant. A change of venue may be requested if the defendant believes that he cannot receive an impartial trial in the location where the crime was committed.

Courts are typically considered to be the core of the criminal justice system. They are the voice of legal authority, they interpret and administer the laws, and they determine the specific rights and duties of citizens. The primary duties of the courts are to convict and sentence the guilty, and to set free the innocent. Courts can be divided into several categories that include lower courts, superior courts, and **appellate courts**. These courts are different in terms of their duties and day-to-day operations.

A Dual Court System

The United States has a dual court system composed of state and federal courts. The typical state court system is made up of three separate subsystems: (1) **courts of limited jurisdiction,** (2) **courts of general jurisdiction**, and (3) appellate courts, which includes state supreme courts, as well as the United States Supreme Court.

THE STATE COURT SYSTEM

Courts of Limited Jurisdiction

There are approximately 13,000 courts of limited jurisdiction in the U.S. They are generally referred to as municipal and lower courts. They are mostly organized at the town, municipal, or county level. Their subject matter includes misdemeanors and small civil suits. They may conduct preliminary hearings in felony court. However, they are restricted in terms of sentencing options. They may include **courts of special jurisdiction,** such as juvenile and family court, or probate court (those that handle the administration of estates and wills).

Courts of General Jurisdiction

There are approximately 3,235 courts of general jurisdiction in the U.S. These courts handle the more serious felony cases and civil matters. They sometimes review appeals from courts of limited jurisdiction.

APPELLATE COURTS

There are approximately 94 appellate courts in the U.S. Each state has at least one supreme court. Many states have intermediate courts. These courts are between-trial courts and **courts of the last resort**. Appellate courts do not retry cases, but rather they review case procedures to determine if mistakes were made at the lower levels. If mistakes were made with respect to constitutional violations, the appellate court has several options that it can invoke which include ordering a new trial, or **trail de nova**, and allowing the defendant to go free. If the appellate court does not find any mistakes made by the lower court, it will uphold the original verdict.

THE FEDERAL COURT SYSTEM

The federal court system has its legal basis in Article III, Section I of the United States Constitution. The federal court system has three tiers that include **district courts**, federal appeal courts, and the U.S. Supreme Court. The federal courts' legal jurisdiction include laws of the United States, treaties, controversies between two states, controversies between citizens of different states, and maritime law, or laws governing the ocean and sea with regard to the navy and marines.

U.S. District Courts

U.S. District Courts are known as **federal trial courts**. A federal trial court is the place where most cases are initially filed and disposed. There are approximately 94 district courts and eighty-nine are located in the fifty states. Their **jurisdiction** includes violations of federal laws, civil rights abuses, interstate transportation of stolen vehicles, kidnaping, citizenship and alien rights, and civil suits. Each state has at least one district court. However, some states may have a northern, southern, eastern, and western or central district. Therefore, such states (California, Texas, New York) have as many as four district courts. This number is contingent upon the size of the state. District courts encompass large geographical areas. Some hold court in various divisions. For example, some districts may have only one division whereas other districts have as many as eight divisions. District courts are also found in the District of Columbia, and four territorial district courts are located in Guam, Puerto Rico, the Virgin Islands, and the Northern Mariana Islands. There are several judges appointed to sit in each district. Cases are heard before a single judge. However, in special federal cases, three judges may sit on the court.

Federal Appeals Courts

These federal courts are also known as U.S. Circuit Courts. They are usually located in major cities. There are thirteen U.S. courts of appeals. For example, the Federal Appeals Court of Missouri is in the Eighth Circuit, which is located in St. Louis. These courts have jurisdiction over several states. The geographical area that a court of appeals covers is called a "circuit." Appeals from the federal district courts are sent to the U.S. Circuit Courts of Appeals. A losing party that contends an error was made in a U.S. district court may file an appeal in a **federal appeals court**. When the appeal is taken, lawyers from each side file briefs arguing the case, in writing and later orally, before the Court of Appeals.

Three judges usually decide the case. One judge writes the opinion of the court. If the judges disagree, the disagreeing judge, or judges, will write the **dissenting opinion** of the court. It is the majority that prevails in the case that the judges are deciding. That opinion becomes the prevailing law, or precedent, on any legal matter that is decided by that case. The important thing is that the decision is binding only in that "circuit" and not in other circuits. However, other courts may look at its conclusion. A federal appeals court reviews federal and state appellate court cases. It also enforces regulatory orders. An appeal must invoke a constitutional guarantee. See Table 1 for a geographical distribution of the U.S. circuits. Only the U.S. Supreme Court can resolve differences between lower federal courts of appeals.

The United States Supreme Court

The U.S. Supreme Court is the only court that is established by constitutional mandate under Article III, Section I. It decides important cases with grave consequences and shapes the meaning of the Constitution. For example, in *Marbury v. Madison* (1803), under Chief Justice John Marshall, the Court established that it was the final authority empowered by the Constitution to invalidate acts of Congress as unconstitutional and that it was the duty of the Court to determine what the law is. In *Marbury*, the Supreme Court asserted its power of **judicial review**. The case is significant because the Constitution does not say that the Supreme Court has the final say on the limitations that the Constitution places on Congress and the President.

The Court has both original and appellate jurisdictions. Therefore, both federal and state cases may reach the Court. The Supreme Court is referred to as the high court and many of its decisions become the basis for public policy. Wasby (1989) argues that, as the highest court, the Supreme Court has the final word in any case involving the Constitution, which is binding on state courts, as well as on federal judges. Despite this finality, the Supreme Court only considers a limited number of cases that have importance to the legal system. The subject matter of the Court is not limited to the matters of criminal justice, but rather the Court decides matters, such as retirement, gay rights, disability, abortions, gun ownership, and other matters that directly impact every aspect of social life. It is referred to as the Court of the last resort. The U.S. Supreme Court has nine justices: One chief justice (William Rehnquist) and eight associates (Anthony Kennedy, David Souter, Clarence Thomas, Ruth Bader Ginsburg, Stephen Breyer, Sandra Day O'Conner, Antonin Scalia, and John Paul Stevens). The members of the Supreme Court are appointed by the President and approved by the Senate. The Court provides direct appeals only for a few cases, such as when a federal or state law is found by a lower court to be unconstitutional. The Court may hear one hundred cases each year. However, before a case can reach the Supreme Court, four of the nine justices must agree to hear the case. This is referred to as the rule of four.

Table 1.

Federal Circuit Courts of Appeals

First Circuit	**Second Circuit**	**Third Circuit**	**Fourth Circuit**
Maine	Connecticut	Delaware	Maryland
Massachusetts	New York	New Jersey	North Carolina
New Hampshire	Vermont	Pennsylvania	South Carolina
Puerto Rico		Virgin Islands	Virginia
Rhode Island			West Virginia
Fifth Circuit	**Sixth Circuit**	**Seventh Circuit**	**Eighth Circuit**
Louisiana	Kentucky	Illinois	Arkansas
Mississippi	Michigan	Indiana	Iowa
Texas	Ohio	Wisconsin	Minnesota
	Tennessee		Missouri
			Nebraska
			North Dakota
			South Dakota
Ninth Circuit		**Tenth Circuit**	**Eleventh Circuit**
Alaska	Montana	Colorado	Alabama
Arizona	Northern Marina Islands	Kansas	Florida
California		New Mexico	Georgia
Guam	Oregon	Oklahoma	
Hawaii	Washington	Utah	
Idaho		Wyoming	
District of Columbia		**Federal** All federal judicial districts	

How Cases Get Selected for Judicial Review

Writ of Error An inquiry made because of an error in law. This is a document issued by a judicial officer ordering, or forbidding, the performance of an act.

Certification Though infrequently used, a lower court faced with a new legal question, instead of resolving the case, "certifies" the question for answer by the Supreme Court. When faced with certification the Court can:

1. refuse the certification, forcing the lower court to decide the question on its own;

2. provide the answer, which the lower court applies; or

3. simply take the case and decide it directly without the extra step of returning it to the lower court.

Appeal A writ issued as a matter of right.

Certiorari An order to a lower court to send up the records in a case; when the Court issues the writ, it has accepted the case. It is granted as a matter of discretion.

Factors Considered in Deciding to Accept an Appeal

Numerous factors may be considered by the Court when deciding to accept an appeal. These may include the following:

A. The highest state court invalidates a federal law or treaty as unconstitutional or upholds a state law or state constitutional provision against a challenge that it violates a federal law, treaty, or the U.S. Constitution.

B. A court of appeals declares a state law or constitutional provision unconstitutional, or declares a federal law unconstitutional when the federal government is a party to a case.

C. A federal district court declares a federal law unconstitutional, again, when the United States is a party or when

D. A three judge district court has granted, or denied, an injunction in cases required to be brought before such a court.

Other factors that may be considered when deciding to grant a review include (1) state statues that conflict with the constitution, (2) the U.S. Constitution, (3) previously decided cases, and (4) a federal question is involved.

Writing the Opinion of the Court

After the Supreme Court hears a case, it must write the opinion of the court. The assignment of writing the opinion of the court is made by the Chief Justice. The opinions include (1) the majority, (2) concurring, and (3) the minority or dissenting opinions. The majority opinion is the decision of the court, or how the case was decided. The **concurring opinion** is the view of those who agreed with the majority's decision in the case but for a different reason. The minority, or dissenting, opinion is the view of those justices who did not agree with the decision of the Court's majority. However, when a case is remanded, it is sent back to the lower court where the case was originally tried. The Court sits in **term of court**. The term runs from October through June. If a justice chooses not to participate or hear a case, he can remove himself from the process.

Federal judges at all levels (district, circuit court, and the U.S. Supreme Court) are appointed by the President of the United States with the advice and consent of the Senate. They serve for life and can be removed only by impeachment. State judges at all levels are elected in most states. In some states, judges are appointed by the Governor, in a few by the legislature, and in some states (lower court judges) by election.

THE FOUNDATION of CRIMINAL LAW

The foundation of criminal law is divided into substantive and procedural law. The law must prohibit an act before it can be regarded as a crime and have accompanying punishment. Substantive law stipulates the types of conduct that are criminal and the punishments to be imposed. Procedural law sets forth the rules that govern the enforcement of the substantive law.

Types of Crime Classification

Crimes are generally classified as either a **felony** or **misdemeanor**. A felony is punishable by more than one year incarceration or a harsher sentence that could include death. It also carries with it certain rights that include a right to counsel for an indigent defendant and a right to a trial by jury. On the other hand, if one is convicted of having committed a felony, he may be barred from specific occupations and professions in various states. Some of the occupations could include medical, legal, police officer, bartender, and becoming a barber. Misdemeanors are punishable by one year or less; often in a local jail, rather than a state prison. The accused may not be entitled to a jury trial. However, he or she must still appear before a judge. If guilt is established, the punishment that he or she faces could be either a fine, penalty, forfeiture, or confinement.

TYPES of LAW -- CRIMINAL and CIVIL

Criminal Law

The most common types of law include criminal and civil. These types of laws follow different rules and procedures in state and federal courts. The criminal law defines an offense against society, and therefore the state punishes the violators. The process is activated by a state official typically referred to as a district attorney or state prosecutor on behalf of all citizens of a particular jurisdiction. The job of the prosecutor is to prove that the accused committed the crime and is guilty beyond a reasonable doubt (level of proof 95%, see Table 2) to win a conviction in court. If the jury is not convinced beyond a reasonable doubt, the jury will probably acquit (set free) the accused, and he or she will be released from custody. Criminal cases are brought by a grand jury or prosecutor (after establishing probable cause -- level of proof +50%) filing state criminal charges. Again, the case is brought by the state against a defendant who is charged with having committed a felony.

Civil Law

Unlike criminal law, civil law defines relationships between individuals within society. Those who are found guilty of a civil wrong are not incarcerated or given the death sentence, but rather directed to pay compensation for their law violation. Civil courts are concerned with compensatory justice for victims who have been harmed, or damaged, by another. The civil law deals with duties owed by one party to another. The two most common types are contracts and torts. **Contract law** is the set of rules that deals with promises made by one person to another. A person may be a corporation, business, or an agency, as well as an individual. On the other hand, **tort law** covers duties owed by one person to another. For example, where injury or harm is caused by one person, a legal remedy may be sought via this action. Both contracts and torts typically seek monetary damages. In some cases involving contracts, injunctive (restrain and free action) relief is sought. In civil law, one needs only to establish a **preponderance of the evidence** to prevail (level of proof +50%, see Table 2) at trial. This may be easier to prove than guilt beyond a reasonable doubt. Civil actions are usually brought by an attorney filing a legal paper (a complaint) on behalf of his client, asking for damages because of injuries and harm sustained. The person bringing the action is the plaintiff, and the person being sued is the defendant.

Class actions are civil cases in which a group of plaintiffs join together in a single class. One plaintiff (or several) is allowed to proceed with the lawsuit on behalf of all involved.

Table 2 reveals a quantification of the levels of proof needed in criminal, as well as civil, proceedings. As indicated, the levels of proof range from (1) **absolute certainty**, (2) beyond a reasonable doubt, (3) **clear and convincing evidence**, (4) probable cause, (5) preponderance of the evidence, (6) reasonable suspicion, (7) reasonable doubt, (8) hunch, to no information. Absolute certainty is rarely achieved in any legal proceeding, since it requires that one is 100 percent convinced that a certain person committed a specific crime. Because this level of proof is difficult to establish, it is not required in any proceeding, criminal or civil. Essentially, one would need a video recording of the entire criminal or civil law violation to establish absolute certainty. Even if this were to occur, the accuracy of what transpired in the video could be challenged and manipulated by both parties involved in the case. Therefore, a video recording of the crime would have to include a showing of both the **actus reus** and the **mens rea** to establish that an individual committed a criminal law violation. As such, absolute certainty is a level of proof that is almost impossible to establish. Proof beyond a reasonable doubt is the legal level of evidence that is used to convict an accused in a criminal trial. When this is established, the jury is virtually saying that it is 95 percent sure that the accused, or defendant, did in fact commit the crime that he or she stands accused of having committed. However, if the public defender, or defense attorney, creates doubt in the mind of the jury through a showing of evidence, the jury is required by law to acquit the defendant of any wrongdoing the state, or prosecutor, is alleging he or she committed. In criminal cases, the lawyer representing the accused only has to create 6 percent of doubt from the evidence that the state has collected to attach criminal responsibility to the defendant.

Clear and convincing evidence is used to deny the defendant bail and the use of the insanity defense. This level of evidence argues that the thing to be proved is highly probable, or reasonably certain. Moreover, a greater burden of proof is required than the preponderance of evidence used in civil court. However, it is less than proof beyond a reasonable doubt that must be established in criminal court. Essentially, one is 80 percent sure that something has happened, or will happen. In the case of granting a suspect bail, judges may rule after a discussion with the prosecutor over the severity of the crime, the suspect's criminal history, and the resources that could enable a defendant to pose a flight risk from the jurisdiction. If it is believed that the crime is nonbailable, bail is usually denied. Furthermore, although the insanity defense is only used successfully in less than one percent of all criminal cases, the insanity plea may be allowed if clear and convincing evidence exists that could negate the element of mens rea.

Probable cause exists when police officers and judges are 50+ percent sure that a suspect committed a particular crime or that incriminating evidence can be found at a specific location. When probable cause is established, police officers file a sworn affidavit alleging that a suspect should be brought in for questioning, or that an item can be retrieved from a specific location. When this is done, judges may issue warrants (it usually takes about 15 minutes to get a warrant from a magistrate, even if it means going to the judge's house), arrests are made by police officers, indictments can be handed down by a grand jury, judges may order a **bill of information**, and searches of persons and seizures of evidence can be made by law enforcement officers. Unlike civil court, probable cause exists in criminal investigations and proceedings.

In civil matters, the preponderance of the evidence is the level of proof that has to be established for plaintiffs to prevail. Preponderance of the evidence means that the complainant must have more, or superior, evidence than the opposing party to win in civil matters. The degree of certainty involved in such cases is +50 percent. Where jurisprudence is concerned, it is not uncommon for victims to lose their cases in criminal court, because the prosecution failed to prove guilt beyond a reasonable doubt, yet prevail in civil court because they have stronger evidence and meet a different standard to establish guilt.

Reasonable suspicion is the level of proof that is needed to justify a stop-and-frisk of a potential suspect. A **stop-and-frisk** is usually conducted to protect the police officer from danger and nothing more. However, reasonable suspicion can turn into probable cause if a frisk leads to the discovery of a weapon or illegal drugs that could lead to an arrest. Reasonable suspicion is achieved when an officer is 20+ percent certain that an individual could be potentially armed with a weapon and therefore poses a serious threat to the safety of an officer or others. Reasonable doubt is established when the local prosecutor, district attorney, or state attorney has failed to convince a jury from the show of evidence that the defendant committed the crime, or crimes, alleged by a particular state or jurisdiction.

Reasonable doubt occurs when the jury is 6 percent certain that the accused did not commit the crime. Because reasonable doubt exists about the defendant's involvement in a crime, the jury is instructed by the presiding judge that it must acquit the accused of committing the crime. When reasonable doubt is achieved, the accused is released and set free from state custody. Hunches and no information have no level of certainty and are tantamount to hearsay evidence. They are, therefore, not sufficient in any proceeding, criminal or civil.

Table 2.

A Quantification of the Levels of Proof, Degree of Certainty, and Proceedings

Level of Proof	Degree of Certainty	Required in Proceedings
Absolute Certainty	100%	Not required in proceedings
Beyond a Reasonable Doubt	95%	To convict an accused
Clear and Convincing Evidence	80%	Deny Bail/Insanity Defense
Probable Cause	+50%	Warrant/Arrest/Indict/Search and Seizure
Preponderance of Evidence	+50%	Civil Cases
Reasonable Suspicion	+50%	Stop and Frisk
Reasonable Doubt	5%	To acquit the accused
Hunch	0%	Not sufficient in any proceeding
No Information	0%	Not sufficient in any proceeding

Table taken from del Carmen, R.V. (1991). Civil Liabilities in American Policing. Englewood Cliffs, New Jersey: Brady Publisher.

Key Terms

acquit
adjudication
appeal
appellate court
appellate jurisdiction
beyond a reasonable doubt
Bill of Rights
case law
certification
certiorari
change of venue
civil law
Code of Hammurabi
concurring opinion
confinement
constitutional law
contract law
corrections
courts of general jurisdiction
courts of limited jurisdiction
courts
criminal law
dissenting opinion
executive orders
family court
federal appeals court
federal court system
felony
fine
forfeiture
Fourteenth Amendment
injunction
injunctive relief
lower court
majority court
minority court
misdemeanor
Mosaic Code
municipal court
penalty
precedent
preponderance of the evidence
probate court
procedural law

regulations of administrative agencies
Rome's Twelve Tables
Rule of Four
selective absorption
selective incorporation
stare decisis
statute law
substantive law
term of court
tort law
treaties
trial de nova
U.S. Circuit Court
U.S. Constitution
U.S. District Court
U.S. Supreme Court
venue
writ of error

CASE CITED

Marbury v. Madison, 5 U.S. (1Cranch) 137 (1803).

REFERENCES

Abraham, H.J. (1988). The Judiciary: The Supreme Court in the Governmental Process. 2nd ed., Dubuque, Iowa: Wm. C. Brown Publishers.

Corwin, E.S., and Peltason, J.W. (1988). Understanding the Constitution. 11th ed., New York: Holt, Rinehart and Winston, Inc.

Cripe, C. A. (1997). Legal Aspects of Corrections Management. Maryland: Aspen Publications.

del Carmen, R. V. (1991). Civil Liabilities in American Policing. Englewood Cliffs, New Jersey: Brady Publishers.

Goldman, S., and Jahnige, T. P. (1985). The Federal Courts as a Political System. 3rd ed., New York: Harper & Row Publishers.

Grilliot, H. J. (1983). Introduction to Law and the Legal System. 3rd ed., Boston: Houghton Mifflin Company.

Spiro, G. W., and Houghteling, J. L. (1981). The Dynamics of Law. 2nd ed., New York: Harcourt Brace Jovanovich, Inc.

Wasby, S. L. (1989). The Supreme Court in the Federal Judicial System. 3rd ed., Chicago: Nelson-Hall Publishers.

CHAPTER 2

The Corrections Component of Criminal Justice

FOCAL POINTS

- What is Corrections?
- Alternatives to Traditional Incarceration Programs
- Secure Confinement
- The Process of Justice
- The Criminal Justice System
- Key Terms

Influenced by Thomas Hobbes, Jean-Jacques Rousseau argued that human nature is bad and man is inherently evil; therefore he must be controlled (Masters, 1978). Social control is defined as the organized way society responds to behavior it regards as deviant, problematic, worrying, threatening, troublesome, or undesirable (Cohen, 1985). Furthermore, Horwitz (1990) argues social control takes many forms, such as punishment, deterrence, treatment, prevention, segregation, justice, rehabilitation, reform, or social defense. Social control is not sinister and does not have to be used in the context of conflict between state officials and citizens. Society has the right to counteract any threat to its survival, otherwise the consequence could be anarchy (Blomberg and Cohen, 1995). The criminal justice system's correctional component addresses this matter. Corrections is the societal right to punish, or correct, those convicted of criminal offenses. Punishment is exercised for four reasons: (1) **incapacitation**, (2) **restitution**, (3) **rehabilitation**, and (4) **retribution** (Murphy, 1995).

There are many offenders who receive various forms of correctional treatments. It is estimated that there are over 1.6 million offenders in places of confinement (640,000 in jails and 998,000 in prisons) and three million offenders on some form of community supervision program, such as **probation** or **parole**. Correctional treatment can be divided into community-based programs, such as regular probation, **intermediate sanctions**, halfway houses, and secure confinement (Clear and Cole, 1994).

Regular Probation

Probation is defined as the suspension of the offender's sentence imposed by a judge in exchange for good behavior in the free community while under supervision. If offenders violate **conditions of probation,** it can be revoked by a judge and the original suspended sentence reimposed. Probationary sentences are designed to extend for specific periods of time and may be granted by state and federal courts. In misdemeanor cases, probation usually extends to the entire period the offender would have been jailed. However, where felonies are concerned, the probationary period is shorter than the sentence the offender would have had to serve in a traditional place of confinement. The success of probation has been questioned because many offenders given this reprieve have recidivated. However, research indicates that offenders placed on probation fare better then those sentenced to prison. As such, it is considered to be a cost-effective means of managing low-risk, or nonserious offenders (Allen, Eskridge, Latessa, and Vito, 1985).

Intermediate Sanctions

Intermediate sanction programs mainly emerged because of prison overcrowding and the low levels of probation supervision. These sanctions are less severe than prison and more restrictive than probation. In other words, offenders sentenced to these sanctions are halfway between the loose supervision of probation and secure confinement. Such sentences are given to law violators who have not engaged in serious felonies and lack extensive criminal histories. They could be first-time offenders who have committed a drug offense. These diversions are given to offenders who are viewed by judicial officials as salvageable and worthy of a second chance to be law-abiding. For this reason, attempts are made to divert these offenders from traditional sentencing and punishment. Intermediate sanction programs are created to reduce **recidivism** and expensive correctional costs, be cost-effective, and free limited bed space for hardened criminals. Some intermediate sanctions are fines; forfeitures; restitution; shock probation and split sentencing; intensive supervision probation; home confinement; residential community corrections; and boot camps (Gorden, 1991). Offenders with a history of violent crimes such as murder, manslaughter, rape, robbery, assault, kidnapping, and prior convictions are excluded from participation in these programs (Clear and Cole, 1994).

Fines

Fines are monetary payments that an offender must pay for his commission of a misdemeanor or felony. Some fines include having to pay for a traffic violation. Other fines are often imposed on offenders based on their ability and means to pay for their criminal infractions or violations (Gorden, 1991). However, fines are rarely used as a sole punishment. They are used in conjunction with other punishments, especially if the defendant has committed a serious crime. It is not unusual for judges to impose a sentence of several years of imprisonment and a fine on offenders. Some argue that this type of penalty is becoming more popular, since many correctional facilities are experiencing prison overcrowding and probation and parole officers are overwhelmed by huge caseloads (Clear and Cole, 1994). Moreover, Champion (1997) contends that fines are financial penalties imposed at the time of sentence on convicted offenders as a sentencing option. It is estimated that over one billion dollars in fines are collected each year by courts across the country. Some of the proceeds from these fines are used to compensate victims.

Forfeiture

A forfeiture is the seizure of assets and goods by the government that are derived from a criminal's involvement in crime. Forfeitures are usually imposed against property acquired from engaging in illegal activities, such as the drug trade (Champion, 1997). Some contend that in contemporary times, the passage of the Racketeer Influence and Corrupt Organizations Act (RICO) and the Continuing Criminal Enterprise Act (CCEA) in 1970 have assisted in the fight against organized crime and the flow of illegal drugs. Forfeiture proceedings can take both a civil and criminal form. Using civil law, property used in criminal activities can be seized without a finding of guilt. Such property typically includes boats, automobiles, houses, and equipment to manufacture illegal drugs. On the other hand, criminal forfeiture is a type of punishment that is imposed by a judge as a result of a conviction (Clear and Cole, 1994). The monetary value taken in asset forfeiture can be astronomical. For example, an estimated one billion dollars worth of assets were confiscated from drug dealings by state and federal officers that occurred over a five-year period that ended in 1990 (New York Times, 1990).

Restitution

Restitution is defined as the repayment to a victim who has suffered some form of financial loss as a direct result of the offender's crime. Restitution is not a new form of punishment; its history extends to the middle ages when compensatory justice was commonplace. Monetary restitution requires that offenders repay those whom they have victimized with money or community services. Champion (1997) contends that restitution is a stipulation by a court that offenders must compensate victims for their financial losses resulting from crime. This could be compensation to a victim for sustaining physical, psychological, or financial loss. Moreover, restitution may be attached as part of a sentence of incarceration (Clear and Cole, 1994). Of the many forms of punishment, restitution is perhaps the most unpublicized, since informal agreements are often made between offender and victim in the presence of law enforcement officials and, at other times, during plea bargaining.

Shock Probation and Split-Sentencing

These programs grant offenders community release after they have sampled prison life. The sentence of imprisonment is meant to shock offenders back into law-abiding behavior. A split-sentence makes jail term a condition of probation. Shock probation involves re-sentencing after a short prison term. The re-sentencing phase usually occurs within 90 days of incarceration (Gorden, 1991). More specifically, an offender receiving shock probation is sentenced to jail or prison for a brief period to be "shocked" by the experience of jail or prison. Afterwards, the offender is released into the custody of a probation or parole officer through a re-sentencing project (Champion, 1997). A split-sentence occurs when a judge orders an offender to serve a sentence for a fixed period of time to be followed by a period of probation for a fixed period.

Intensive Probation Supervision

An intensive supervision probation program is based on control and intensive supervision. In the programs, offenders (probationers or parolees) are subjected to a set of rules and regulations that are referred to as technical conditions of release. A violation of any condition could mean that the offender will be sentenced to a traditional place of secured confinement. The probation officer to offender ratio is very low, allowing many contact visits and meaningful monitoring of the participants' progress. Some of the conditions include observing curfew, random drug test, close contact with probation officers, employment, school, counseling, community service, and others. The program is designed to reintegrate the offender back into the community (Gorden, 1991). Criticisms have emerged that question if constant surveillance is enough to reform offenders. Critics argue that though these programs are designed to reintegrate offenders back into society, offenders complain of not being able to find employment opportunities and not receiving family and drug counseling.

Home Confinement and Electronic Monitoring

Home confinement requires that offenders spend extended periods of time in their own home. While at home, offenders are allowed to maintain employment, if they have a job. However, they must return home by a specified time. Home confinement is usually administered by the probation department. Home confinement, or house arrest, has gained increasing attention because of the growing number of offenders in places of confinement. Because of prison overcrowding, home confinement has served as a viable alternative to secure confinement. But this sanction is not for every offender. This type of sentence might be more appropriate for "special needs" offenders, those who are pregnant, disabled, elderly, HIV/AIDS infected, and so on. On the other hand, offenders with a history of violence, sale of drugs or stolen property would not be good candidates for this program (Anderson, 1999). Nevertheless, there is little evidence of the effectiveness of this sanction. Furthermore, officials use either random calls or make visits to ensure compliance of house arrest. Another way to ensure that the offender complies is the use of electronic monitoring. Where electronic monitoring is concerned, there are two types of technologies: active and passive. The active technology sends continuous signals to a central headquarters. Passive technology involves a random call that is computer-generated (Gorden, 1991).

Residential Community Centers

Residential Community Centers (RCC) entail the usage of a halfway house that emphasizes the goals of reintegration and control of the offender (Gorden, 1991). These programs require that the offender lives on the premises while working in the community. Living in the center, participants are often provided with a number of therapeutic treatments that are design to ensure a successful reintegration into society. The participants in these centers usually receive individual and drug counseling. Part of the strategy used by RCC is to create an environment that is exactly like a home (e.g., bed, dinning, and living rooms, kitchen). As such, many centers are renovated homes or hotels. Counselors believe that such an environment is needed for a healthy adjustment after release. More specifically, this correctional approach deals with sentencing an offender to a halfway house or other community home where the offender, or client, may come and go freely during daytime hours for work or education. The clients must return to the community home by evening hours to observe curfew. Despite this reasonable arrangement, these centers face a number of problems, such as high staff turnover rate, expensive operational costs, high failure rate, and more. And if an offender commits a crime in the community, there is public outcry that the center must be closed because offenders pose a threat to community safety (Clear and Cole, 1994). In many cases, offenders are required to pay for their room and board with money they earn from working in the community.

Boot Camp Programs

Boot camps are referred to as shock incarceration programs. These programs tend to target young first-time offenders by imposing on them a strict paramilitary regime for a period of 90 to 180 days, depending on whether the offender is recycled for failure to make satisfactory progress in all phases of the program. Offenders are subjected to discipline, exercise, physical fitness, drills and ceremonies, hard work, counseling treatment approaches, and the opportunity to earn a high school equivalence diploma and learn technical skills that will be helpful upon release. The overall effectiveness of boot camps is unknown, because while each boot camp program has similar components, they are operated and implemented differently by prison officials (Anderson, Dyson, and Burns, 1999). Yet, boot camps, in general, have come under serious attack in recent times. Because of the death of one participant and the verbal and physical abuse of others, one boot camp was ordered to close by the Governor of Maryland.

Secure Confinement

Jails or detention facilities are secure institutions that are used to house offenders prior to trial and house misdemeanants sentenced for one year or less. Jail conditions are poor and in need of reform. They lack a classification system and house violent, as well as nonviolent, offenders. Prisons are places that house offenders who have received a sentence of over one year for having committed a felony. Because offenders are not in jail for extended periods of time, jails act only as holding cells and do not offer any rehabilitation programs. Though most jails across the country are similar, there are different types of prisons, such as maximum, medium, and minimum security. **Maximum security prisons** have elaborate security measures and armed guards to house dangerous offenders. **Medium security prisons** operate without armed guards or walls and house less serious violent inmates. **Minimum security prisons** have little preventive measures, and inmates are allowed to have some personal items that maximum offenders are not allowed (Duffee, 1989). The type of prison to which an offender is sentenced is contingent upon the criminal activity in which he engaged. The typical prison inmate in America is a poor, young, adult male with less than a high school education. Today's inmates are disproportionately African-Americans (Duffee, 1989).

Private prisons are also a growing phenomenon in the United States. They are often referred to as **prisons for profit**. They are used by several states (e.g., Texas, Florida, and Kentucky) and the federal government. The biggest criticisms of private prisons are over security and the types of offenders being housed in these private facilities.

Parole

Parole is the planned release and community supervision of incarcerated offenders before the expiration of a prison sentence. The decision to grant **parole** is decided by statutory requirement and granted by a **parole board**. Some states use discretionary parole in which the decision is made at a parole grant hearing. The accumulation of "good time" reduces minimum sentences and quickens parole consideration. The parolee is assisted with his reintegration into society by a parole officer who helps him adjust to the community and find employment. The continuation of parole is contingent on the released adherence to **conditions of parole**. For example, if the conditions of parole are violated, parole can be revoked. Many parolees are rearrested for committing new crimes, as well as violating technical conditions of release (Allen, Eskridge, Latessa, and Vito, 1985). Parolees are under the supervision of corrections.

The Process of Justice

In the United States, the criminal justice system is responsible for dispensing justice to its citizens. Justice is served when a person is given what is due to him according to standards of the law. The law is rooted in constitutional rights, civil liberties, and safeguards designed to ensure that people will not be the victims of governmental oppression. Therefore, agents of the justice system must conform their conduct to standards of the law. The laws that guide the behaviors of the justice system include the U.S. Constitution, state constitutions, and other legal codes. Though the responsibility of meting out justice falls on the justice agencies or the agencies of social control, sometimes it is difficult to provide this function in a multi-cultural society. Despite this difficulty, justice must be dispensed with impartially while ensuring the greatest protection of due process and equal protection of the laws. The components of the criminal justice system include police, courts, prosecution, correction, and the juvenile justice system. They are responsible for ensuring fairness and equity guaranteed by both federal and state constitutions. Indeed, the criminal justice system is charged with balancing **individual rights** with the **public order mandate**. Individual rights are those rights that individuals have while facing criminal prosecution. The public order mandate is that which demands protecting public safety.

The Criminal Justice System

A system is defined as a group of components working together for a common goal. Systems are characterized as having inputs, transformation processes, outputs, and eventually feedback to influence the next selection of inputs to enter into the system. The dynamics that occur within a system are characterized by interrelations, interdependency, and interactions (Burrell and Morgan, 1979; Argyris, 1980; Churchman, 1979). This presupposes that the elements in the system have direct contact and interactions with each other. Moreover, system theory holds that any thing that affects one component or part of the system will affect the entire operation. Churchman (1979) argues that the systems approach is simply a way of thinking about the total systems and their components. This is not true of criminal justice. There are three primary components in the criminal justice system that include police, court, and corrections. Though they are responsible for dispensing justice, these components rarely have close contact with each another and almost never have similar goals. Systems are influenced by their internal and external environments. The internal environment is impacted by leadership styles, manpower, and resources. The external environment is shaped by the social, political, and legal climates. Some believe that because of this dualism, police, courts, and corrections have different goals and objectives. There is no consensus on what the end result, or finished product (offender), should be. Instead, there is hardly any interaction between police and correctional officials. The same can be said for police and courts, with the exception of police testimony about a defendant during the criminal trial -- if the case is not plea bargained, which occurs 89 percent of the time (Gaines, Kaune, and Miller, 2000).

Though the justice agencies are referred to as a criminal justice system, they are at best a loose connection of independent agencies. For example, there are two competing models that are used to explain the criminal justice system. They are the consensus and conflict models. The **consensus model** makes the argument that the subcomponents in the criminal justice system work together harmoniously to achieve justice. It is considered the most acceptable view among the majority of criminal justice experts, as well as employees, in the justice system. However, the **conflict model** argues the contrary. According to the conflict model, each subcomponent of the criminal justice system functions to serve its own interest. Moreover, it contends that justice is produced from conflict among the agencies within the system that results from cooperation among component agencies. Similarly, Frost (1977) agrees, but takes the analysis a step further, arguing that criminal justice cannot truly function in the capacity of a system. More specifically, he contends that the strength of the American system of criminal justice rests on the notion of the **separation of powers** and the independence of outside interference. He argues that a centralized uniform system of criminal justice would be unconstitutional. The diagram below is a model of the criminal justice system.

Figure 1.

The Criminal Justice System

Feedback

The process of justice is contingent on the effectiveness of police, courts, and corrections. For example, the police are charged with reducing and preventing crime. However, rare is the occasion when officers happen on crimes in progress. When they can, officers make a formal arrest by taking suspects into custody to answer charges for having committed crimes. Upon arrival to the police station, suspects are booked. The booking process involves making an official entry, or record, of the suspect's arrest. The process includes taking a photograph of the suspect, taking fingerprints, and obtaining general information about the crime and personal information about the suspect. Because they literally bring offenders into the system, police are considered the "gatekeepers" of the criminal justice system. Prosecutors represent the interests of the state. They bring charges against those who are allegedly guilty of having committed crimes. Police typically collect evidence from crime scenes to help prosecutors establish cases against those defendants who are believed to be the perpetrators of crime. In states that have a grand jury system, prosecutors can go before them to present evidence showing that a suspect has committed a crime. The prosecutor tries to convince the jury that there is evidence linking a particular person to a specific crime. The intent is to convinced the grand jury, through a show of evidence, to issue a **bill of indictment**.

If the grand jury finds probable cause to believe that a suspect did, in fact, commit the crime, the grand jury will issue a **true bill**, which means that the grand jury is satisfied that the suspect committed the crime and, therefore, the prosecutor prepares to take the case to trial. If the grand jury returns a **no bill**, it is not satisfied that a suspect committed a crime and the defendant is set free. In states where there is no grand jury system, the prosecutor initiates an accusation that a suspect committed a crime and provides evidence that links the suspect to the crime. If the judge finds that probable cause exists, the case goes to trial and the offender is further processed. If the judge finds probable cause wanting, the suspect is freed. Assuming that the suspect is tried and found guilty, he or she faces the imposition of being sentenced by the judge. This occurs after a **pre-sentence investigation**. Pre-sentence investigations are conducted to determine information about the defendant. The result of the investigation could influence the sentencing judge, provided that there are no mandatory sentences associated with the crime committed by the defendant. When the judge imposes sentence, it can be either probation, an intermediate sanction, fine, or a sentence to a traditional place of confinement. Despite the sentence imposed, it will most likely invoke the last component in the justice system -- corrections.

Recent statistics reveal that there are over 1.6 million inmates in jails and prisons and over three million offenders are under community supervision as either probationers or parolees. The corrections component deals with carrying out the sentence, or punishment, given to the defendant by the court. The **department of corrections** deals with those who receive a traditional sentence of imprisonment and the **department of probation** with those who are either serving a sentence of probation or parole in the free community. The department of corrections provides custody for those facing confinement, and supervision for those facing controlled supervision in the community. The bulk of this book will address the rights of people in secure confinement -- prisoners.

Key Terms

active technology
bill of indictment
bill of information
boot camps
community-based programs
community supervision programs
corrections
courts
criminal justice system

electronic monitoring
day fine
Department of Corrections
Department of Probation
fine
forfeiture
home confinement
incapacitation
intermediate sanctions
intensive supervision probation program
jails
juvenile justice system
maximum security prison
medium security prison
minimum security prison
monetary restitution
no bill
parole
parolee
passive technology
police
pre-sentence investigation
prisons
private prison
probation
probation officer
prosecution
rehabilitation
residential community
restitution
retribution
shock incarceration programs
shock probation
split sentence
sentence

REFERENCES

Allen, H. E., Eskridge, C. W., Latessa, E. J., and Vito, G. F. (1985). Probation and Parole in America. New York: The Free Press.

Anderson, J. F. (1999). "Is Electronic Monitoring A Successful Community Supervision Method." Pp. 39-56 in Controversial Issues in Corrections. Charles Fields (Ed.) Boston: Allyn & Bacon Publishers.

Anderson, J. F., Dyson, L., and Burns, J. C. (1999). Boot Camps: An Intermediate Sanction. Maryland: University Press of America.

Blomberg, T. G., and Cohen, S. (1995). (Eds.). Punishment and Social Control. New York: Aldine De Gruyter.

Burrell, G., and Morgan, G. (1979). Sociological Paradigms and Organizational Analysis. Heinemann, London.

Champion, D.J. (1997). The Roxbury Dictionary of Criminal Justice: Key Terms and Major Court Cases. Los Angeles, CA: Roxbury Publishing Company.

Churchman, C. W. (1979). The Systems Approach. New York: A Delta Book.

Clear, T.D., and Cole, G. F. (1994). American Corrections. 3rd ed. Belmont, CA: Wadsworth Publishing Company.

Cohen, S. (1985). Visions of Social Control. Cambridge: Polity Press.

Duffee, D. E. (1989). Corrections: Practice and Policy. New York: Random House Press.

Frost, M. L., (1979). "To What Extent Should the Criminal Justice System be a System?" Crime and Delinquency. 23 (4): 403.

Gaines, L., Kaune, M, and Miller, R. L. (2000). Criminal Justice in Action. Belmont, CA: Wadsworth/Thompson Learning.

Gorden, D. R. (1991). The Justice Juggernaut: Fighting Street Crime, Controlling Citizens. New Brunswick: Rutgers University Press.

Horwitz, A. V. (1990). The Logical of Social Control. New York: Plenum Press.

Masters, R. D. (1978). (Eds). Jean-Jacques Rousseau: On the Social Contract with Geneva Manuscript and Political Economy. New York: St. Martins's Press.

Murphy, J. G. (1995). Punishment and Rehabilitation. 3rd ed. Belmont, CA: Wadsworth Publishing Company.

CHAPTER 3

From Hands-off to Hands-on

FOCAL POINTS

- The Hands-off Approach
- *Ruffin v. Commonwealth*
- The Black Muslim Movement
- *Copper v. Pate*
- The Hands-on Approach
- Key Terms

Prior to the 1960s, conditions in places of confinement were insufferable. The courts literally took a hands-off approach when it came to addressing the problems and concerns of prisoners (Feely and Rubin, 1998). During this time, the complaints and conditions of inmates went ignored. Goffman (1961) argued that inmates' status put them outside of the law, and there was no way to protest conditions of imprisonment, because communication with the outside world was curtailed and appellate courts, even if reached, would rarely respond to inmates' petitions. The courts, in general, and judges in particular, were of the opinion that prison administrations knew more about the operations of prisons then they. Some scholars argued that judges accepted the reality that they were not penologists and felt that their intervention would only serve to disrupt the discipline that was common to places of confinement (Clear and Cole, 1994). Other scholars maintained that many judges were, in fact, faced with a lack of knowledge where correctional concerns emerged, but were also guided by the precedents of *Ruffin v. Commonwealth* (1871). In *Ruffin,* a Virginia court said that a prisoner, as a consequence of his crime, not only forfeited his liberty but also his personal rights, except those which the law in its humanity accords to him. He, for the time being, is a slave to the state. As a result, prison administrators and wardens exercised complete power and control that went unquestioned and unchallenged (Dilulio, 1987). Judges deferred to the expertise of prison administrators.

Prisoners served their sentences at the will and pleasure of the warden. Inmates had no avenue to seek relief from conditions of confinement, even if the conditions were inhumane. It was not uncommon for inmates to experience serious physical and psychological violence at the hands of prison officials, as well as elite inmates chosen by the warden to assist in controlling prison security. **Elite prisoners** were elevated to this status, because they provided essential information needed to promote greater internal security among the inmate population. Moreover, some correctional settings had more elite prisoners than correctional guards who helped maintain control and the operations of prisons. Furthermore, many inmates were denied the opportunity to exercise their religious beliefs. Others were denied the most basic standard of medical care and treatment. Some inmates were placed in solitary confinement for extended periods of time without being afforded **due process of law**, and a chance to defend themselves against alleged rule infractions. Even as late as 1951, a federal judge articulated the prevailing attitudes towards entertaining complaints of inmates. In *Stroud v. Swope* (1951), the Ninth Circuit Court argued, "We think that it is well settled that it is not the function of the court to superintend and provide treatment and discipline of persons in penitentiaries, but only to deliver from imprisonment those who are illegally confined."

Correctional scholars agree that the Civil Rights Movement of the 1960s spilled over into places of confinement. Many minority prison groups (the Black Panthers and the Black Muslims) began to complain about many of the same injustices that they were experiencing in the free society. They complained of being denied due process and equal protection of the laws. The struggle for civil and human rights captured the attention of the liberal Supreme Court under Chief Justice Earl Warren, along with groups such as the **American Civil Liberties Union**. Moreover, various legal service agencies began to provide legal counsel to prisoners and to argue for the redress of inmates' grievances. As these events unfolded, inmates began to have their voices heard with respect to challenging the conditions of their confinement (Cole, 1995). The one case that signaled a move from the hands-off approach was *Copper v. Pate* (1964). In *Copper*, the Court ruled that prisoners were entitled to the protections of the Civil Rights Act of 1871. This legislation, referred to as Section 1983, imposes civil liability on anyone acting under **color of law** who deprives someone in their custody of a constitutional right or federal protection. In *Copper*, the federal courts recognized that prisoners could sue state officials over the conditions of their confinement. Any constitutional violation would provide cause to invoke Section 1983 as a legal remedy. Actions such as brutality by guards, inadequate nutritional and medical care, theft of personal property, and the denial of basic rights that has been so commonplace were now actionable under this remedy (Cole, 1995). *Copper*, in essence, reduced the amount of power and control that correctional administrators once enjoyed and eventually defined aspects of correctional administration. *Copper* was the beginning of the hands-on era of prison litigation.

With the hands-on approach, the American Bar Association Joint Committee on the Legal Status of Prisoners (1977) reported:

> Prisoners retain all the rights of free citizens except those on which restriction is necessary to assure their orderly confinement or to provide reasonable protection for the rights and physical safety of all members of the prison community.

Since prisoners retain many rights enjoyed by people in the free community, the American Bar Association stated that three governmental interests may justify prison regulations that limit prisoners' rights. They are those that are created to (1) preserve order and discipline, (2) protect against prison escape, and (3) help in the rehabilitation of the offender. As such, any prison policy that is designed to accomplish one or all of the following justifications will prevail even if the regulation infringes on a Constitutionally-established right. Essentially, when a case comes before the Court, it conducts a balancing test that examines prisoners' rights and governmental interests. These cases are determined on a case-by-case basis. The prison administration only has to ask, "Does the policy or penal regulation help to accomplish one of the three justifications of an infringement of an inmate's constitutional rights?" Unlike the past, the burden of establishing the necessity of a regulation is now on the penal administration. In the past, officials operated prisons the way they saw fit. Since the acceptance of a hands-on approach by the courts, inmates enjoy the same freedoms as people in the free community, with the exceptions of restrictions that are needed by correctional institutions to protect internal order and security, prevent escape, and promote the rehabilitation of prisoners (del Carmen, 1991).

When the hands-on approach took effect, several entire state prison systems were declared as operating unconstitutionally. In nearly every state there were discoveries of individual prisons operating in violation of established constitutional protections. Nearly every prison had litigation pending that challenged conditions of confinement, especially prison overcrowding. As a result, nearly every state had prisons that were operating under federal court order to alleviate unconstitutional conditions. Court orders typically direct prison wardens to lower the number of prisons in their facilities to reduce prison overcrowding, upgrade the physical conditions of places of confinement, increase the number of correctional guards, upgrade the quality of food services, and provide adequate medical facilities. Since the 1970s, federal judges in nearly every state have been active in ordering reforms of prisons. These federal court orders have been significant in transforming the conditions of confinement (Chilton, 1991; Crouch and Marquart, 1990; Taggart, 1989; and Feeley, 1989). As late as 1992, Corrections Digests reported that forty states, plus the District of Columbia, Puerto Rich, and the U.S. Virgin Islands, were under a consent decree to limit populations and improve conditions of confinement. Some of these court orders apply to entire correctional systems and others focus on major institutions. In many states, the federal courts have appointed a special master, or monitor, who supervises the management of correctional facilities while they move towards compliance with court orders (see Chapter Five for discussion).

Key Terms

American Bar Association
American Bar Association Joint
  Committee on the Legal Status of Prisoners
American Civil Liberties Union
elite prisoners
hands-off approach
hands-on approach

CASES CITED

Copper v. Pate, 378 U.S. 546 (1964).
Ruffin v. Commonwealth, 62 Va. 790 (1871).
Stroud v. Swope, 187 F.2d 850 (9th Cir. 1951).

REFERENCES

American Bar Association Joint Committee on the Legal Status of Prisoners (1977). "Standards Relating to the Legal Status of Criminals." American Criminal Law Review 14.

Chilton, B. (1991). Prisons Under the Gavel: The Federal Takeover of Georgia Prisoners. Columbus: Ohio State University Press.

Clear, T. R., and Cole, G. F. (1994). American Corrections. 3rd ed. Belmont, CA: Wadsworth Publishing Company.

Cole, G. F.. (1995). The American System of Criminal Justice. 3rd ed. Boston: Wadsworth Publishing Company.

Crouch, B., And Marquart, J. (1990). "Resolving the Paradox of Reform: Litigation, Prisoner Violence and Perceptions of Risk." Justice Quarterly, 7:103-123.

del Carmen, R. V., (1991). Civil Liabilities in American Policing. Englewood Cliffs, NJ: Prentice Hall.

Dilulio, J. J. (1987). Governing Prisons: A Comparative Study of Correctional Management. New York: The Free Press.

Feeley, M. (1989). "The Significance of Prison Conditions Cases: Budgets and Regions.: Law and Society Review, 23: 273-282.

Feeley, M., and Rubin, E. L. (1998). Judicial Policymaking and the Modern State. Cambridge, U.K.: Cambridge University Press.

Goffman, E. (1961). Asylum. Garden City, NY: Anchor Press.

New York Times, 16 July 1990.

Taggart, W. (1989). "Redefining the Power of the Federal Judiciary: The Impact of Court-Ordered Prison Reform on State Expenditures for Corrections." Law and Society Review, 23: 241-272.

The National Prison Project (1992). "Status Report: State Prisons and the Courts." Corrections Digest. March 19: 3-9.

CHAPTER 4

Types of Lawsuits and Petitions Brought by Inmates

FOCAL POINTS

- Tort Suits
- Civil Rights Act or Section 1983
- State Constitutional Rights Act
- Habeas Corpus
- Civil Rights of Institutionalized Persons Act
- Key Terms

When issues emerge in places of confinement where inmates believe they have standings to bring a suit or challenge an existing regulation or practice, they have several remedies available to them. The type of remedy for which they opt is contingent on the issue before them. Some common law suits and actions that inmates bring for relief include (1) tort suits, (2) Civil Rights Act or Section 1983, (3) State Constitutional Rights Actions (4), Habeas Corpus, and (5) Civil Rights of Institutionalized Persons Act.

Tort Suits

A **tort** is a private wrong or injury for which a court will provide a remedy in the form of damages or compensation. The relief given in a tort action is an award of money. There is no **injunctive relief** in a tort suit, and **attorney fees** are not usually given in common law torts. It always and **attorney fees** are not usually given in common law torts. It always involves a violation of some duty owed to the injured person. There are three elements found in any tort action. First is a **legal duty** owed by the defendant to the plaintiff. Second is a breach of that duty. Third is an injury, or damage, caused as a result of the breach of that duty. Stated another way, in order for a tort action to be initiated, there must be an established duty, a breach of such a duty, and an injury sustained because of the breach.

TYPES OF TORTS

There are three different categories of state torts based on the person's conduct. These include (1) intentional, (2) negligence, and (3) **strict liability torts**. First, in a correctional setting, **intentional torts** occur when there is intention on the part of an officer to bring either physical or psychological harm or damage to a prisoner. In correctional settings, several kinds of intentional torts are often brought against penal officials. Perhaps the main claim brought against officials is the use of excessive force. Second, **negligence tort** is defined as the breach of a common law or statutory duty to act reasonably toward those who may foreseeably be harmed by one's conduct. Negligence tort applies in many aspects of correctional work. Third, strict liability tort is a type of action that never occurs in correctional settings and is rarely invoked in the free community. It is concerned with liability that does not depend on actual negligence or intent to harm but rather is based on the breach of an absolute duty to make something safe. Strict liability tort mostly applies either to ultra-hazardous activities or in product liability cases. The most common actions that will prompt a tort violation include assaults, battery, false imprisonment, libel, and defamation.

Damages

There are three types of damages that may be recovered in a civil tort suit. These are compensatory, punitive, and nominal damages (some states do not allow punitive damages in tort actions). First, **compensatory damages** are awarded to the plaintiff. These include (a) repair to property, if it was damaged, and (b) personal injury, such as medical bills, lost wages, pain and suffering, and even future earnings. Second, **punitive damages** are designed to punish the defendant for engaging in severely bad conduct. In these cases, the prison official or correctional guard must have acted or shown recklessness or willful negligence (acting intentionally to cause harm). This intent must be established to justify the issuance of punitive damages. Third, **nominal damages** are those that are relatively small in that very little money is awarded. This occurs when a tort has technically been committed, but the judge and jury are not satisfied that serious injury has been sustained. The judge, or jury, decides that a small monetary award is in the best interest of both parties.

Civil Rights Act or Section 1983

The overwhelming number of lawsuits filed by inmates comes from Section 1983 actions. However, in order to have a legitimate claim under this action, the plaintiff must establish that a person, acting under the color of state law, caused a violation of his constitutional or federal rights. What is important to know about Section 1983 litigation is that the action can only be brought by a person and cannot be brought against the state. The action can only be brought against state employees.

The Civil Rights Act or Section 1983 states:

> Every person, under the color of any statue, ordinance, regulation, subject or causes to be subject, any citizens of the United States or other person within the jurisdiction there of to the deprivation of any rights, privileges, or immunities secured by the Constitution and laws, shall be liable to the party involved in an action at law, suit in equity, or other proper proceeding for redress.

Before discussing the Civil Rights Act, a brief discussion of the elements is needed. These include color of law, action, personal involvement, and liability.

Color of Law

Lawsuits can be brought against state government employees for actions arising out of their employment, i.e., employees acting "under the color of law." Such employees are typically law enforcement, as well as correctional officers.

Action

In order to have a claim, there must be a violation of a constitutional right or a violation of a federal statutory right. A violation of a federal statute is a rare occurrence in correctional litigation, since very few federal statutes protect inmates.

Personal Involvement

In order to be liable, a defendant must have actually participated in or caused the constitutional violation. This area has changed in recent times to include supervisors and administrators who should have had knowledge of such violations.

Liability May Not Be Imposed

Liability cannot simply be attached because the defendant whose direct actions caused the violation, has some supervisory authority over the individual.

Supervisory Liability

Section 1983 claims impose liability when someone "causes one to be subjected to a constitutional violation." The courts are now focusing on supervisory personnel who do not directly participate in such violations (actions or omissions). Recent cases that have imposed supervisor liability have centered around the failure to supervise and to adequately train employees. First, the failure to supervise occurs when a supervisory staff member has knowledge of a pattern of constitutionally offensive actions, but fails to take remedial actions to prevent the continuation of the acts. The Court has said that liability may be attached if the supervisor's action or omission can be said to be "deliberately indifferent" to the constitutional rights of the victim or prisoner. For example, a supervisor has witnessed prisoners being severely beaten by correctional guards on many occasions. A judge and jury may find that the supervisor supported, or condoned, the use of excessive force and, at the same time, showed a **deliberate indifference** to the plight of inmates. Second, the failure to train can be asserted if it is serious enough to show "deliberate indifference" to the constitutional rights of someone. When this occurs, supervisors may be held liable. Typically, prison administrators or supervisors may assign a new staff member to a constitutionally sensitive position, with full knowledge that the person given the assignment is untrained in the constitutional issues involved in the work assignment. Sometimes a "failure to train" claim may be brought regarding matters of improper supervision or assignment, gross failures in hiring and retention, and failures in directing staff. These lawsuits can be very expensive.

Forms of Relief Under the Civil Rights Act

There are two varieties of relief that prisoners can seek under claims of Section 1983. These are injunctions and damages. Injunctive relief is an order from the court to a defendant that requires the defendant to stop performing a particular practice. The failure to comply with the court order could mean that the defendant will face potential sanctions, such as being held in contempt of court. The punishment could mean having to pay a fine or facing the prospect of imprisonment. Damages are monetary awards. These awards can be small or very large for prisoners if they can established that they suffered a constitutionally protected violation of their rights and demonstrate that the official was acting under color of law. However, defendants can prevail in court if they can show that a right allegedly violated was not "clearly established." Accomplishing this, they may be granted qualified immunity, and thus cannot be required to pay damages. This practice is essentially known as exercising the **"good faith" exception**. When officers or administrators assert the good faith defense, they are asserting that they thought, at the time of the infraction, they were acting within the scope of the law. Therefore, the focus is shifted from the employees' state of mind and is placed on the "state of the law at the time." Again, the question is whether the law was "clearly established" at the time of the infraction. The defense only protects employees, and not governmental agencies. If the defense is successful, it can only protect the employee against having to pay damages, not against injunctive relief. If the court finds that certain practices are unfair, they must stop.

Types of Damages Under Section 1983 Litigations

There are four types of damages under Section 1983. They are nominal, compensatory, punitive, and attorney fees. Nominal damages are given to a plaintiff whose rights were violated, but whose actual harm is unproven. Unfortunately, in these instances, the courts have consistently said that defendants are only entitled to one dollar. Compensatory damages are given for injuries that the plaintiffs usually suffer. These could include factors, such as lost wages and medical expenses. In many cases, they include losses, such as pain and suffering, and in other cases, mental anguish. Punitive damages are intended to punish those who engage in unlawful behavior to deter them, and potentially others, from engaging in similar behavior in the future. These awards are typically given when defendants knowingly violate the constitutional rights of plaintiffs. Attorney fees are given to the prevailing party in these civil actions. Sparked by the Attorney Fees Act, they primarily benefit the prevailing plaintiffs, since the law has been interpreted to allow fees for prevailing defendants only when the plaintiffs' actions can be shown to have been frivolous or careless.

Reasons Inmates Prefer to File Civil Rights Suits

There are several reasons why prisoners are attracted to Section 1983 litigations. They include the following three reasons, even when the burden of proof in these cases may be greater than that in tort suits, which require a preponderance of the evidence (the majority or +50 percent):

(1) Historically, federal courts have been more receptive and sympathetic than state courts regarding the plight of those in places of confinement.

(2) No injunctive relief is available in a tort action, and sometimes state law places limitations on the amount of damages that can be awarded against government officials.

(3) Attorney fee awards are available in civil rights cases. These are not provided in tort claims.

Although Section 1983 only covers state employees and cannot be used to bring suit against federal officials, the Court has asserted in *Bivens v. Six Unknown Agents of the Federal Bureau of Narcotics (1971)* that federal officials can be sued in a manner similar to that set forth at USCA 1983 for state officials who violate a person's constitutional rights under the color of state law. Stated another way, Bivens is used the same as Section 1983 in that it applies to federal officials acting under color of law.

Recent Changes to Section 1983 Claims

Some argue that the Prison Litigation Reform Act of 1995, though signed into law in 1996, has changed prison litigation in the federal courts. The Court has now stated that suits cannot be used to challenge prison conditions until administrators have exhausted all available remedies. According to the Act:

> No action shall be brought with respect to prison conditions under Section 1983 by a prisoner confined in any jail, prison, or other correctional facility until such administrative remedies as are available are exhausted.

While the Act represented this strong position, it also placed other limitations on prisoners' lawsuits. For example, (1) it allows for the dismissal of frivolous suits without requiring exhaustive remedies; (2) it places limitations on attorney fees; (3) it requires inmates seeking to proceed without funds to show proof of a lack of funds; (4) it limits orders of relief to change prison conditions to address only a particular violation; (5) it limits consent decrees in scope; and (6) it limits the use of special masters. Many correctional experts and legal scholars believe that these new additions to Section 1983 claims will serve to reduce the number of state prisoners' rights claims brought to court, because many will not progress beyond the administrative remedies.

State Constitutional Rights Act

The State Constitutional Rights Act provides inmates redress when violations of state constitutional protections occur. They are typically directed at the state employee, or agency, responsible for the violation. These claims are filed in state courts. However, if a federal violation has been committed, the claim could be taken to federal court. Inmates filing such claims normally ask for remedies, such as damages (compensation), injunctions, and declaratory relief.

Habeas Corpus

In habeas corpus actions the petitioner claims that he is being illegally held in violation of some constitutional right. These claims are filed by people in places of confinement. The main issue in these cases is the legality of imprisonment. This remedy is not concerned with establishing the guilt of an inmate, nor is it seen as a means of an appeal. That is something that will be decided, if not already decided, in a court of law. The right to petition the government for illegal detainment is found in Article IX of the U.S. Constitution. When these claims are filed, the prisoner (petitioner) completes a petition for habeas corpus and submits it to the court in hope that the court will find cause to grant a Writ of Habeas Corpus granting freedom to the inmate. If the court grants *The Great Writ*, it essentially instructs the jailer, or warden (respondent), to bring the person who is confined before the court and show cause for the detainment. In essence, the court asks the respondent to show why a writ of habeas corpus should not be issued to the petitioner. These matters are typically expedited in about ten days or less (Cripe, 1997). After the attorney for the respondent replies to the court, the court can exercise one of the following options: (1) dismiss the petition because of a show of cause for detainment, (2) order a hearing to obtain more information about the circumstances of the detainment, or (3) grant the request and issue the writ. The latter occurs when there is a lack of cause for the detention of the petitioner. Although habeas corpus cases seldom succeed, they give prisoners another judicial avenue to pursue when they feel that they have been wrongly convicted and imprisoned.

Relief in Habeas Corpus Cases

Relief in habeas corpus cases is release from the custody of jail or prison. This remedy does not provide for the award of damages, but instead is seen as a tool by lawyers for assisting inmates under the death sentence to challenge the appropriateness of that status (Cripe, 1997). Despite the traditional use of the writ, it has, in recent times, been used to achieve release from certain types of confinement, such as illegal segregation. It is important to note here that if the petitioner is successful in requesting removal from illegal segregation, he or she is not entitled to be released from prison custody completely; he or she simply goes back into the general population with other inmates. As a general rule, federal courts have been reluctant to get involved in matters of habeas corpus involving state prisoners, but instead, believe that the appropriate court may be in the state system.

The Decline of Habeas Corpus

Cheurprakobkit and Theis (1999) argue that though habeas corpus was established to allow the federal courts to review the actions of state courts with respect to convictions and sentencing, in recent times, the federal courts have placed limitations on the number of successive petitions that can be brought by state inmates. Furthermore, the federal courts have implemented a retroactive threshold requirement, a procedural default standard, and a full and fair rule. Cheurprakobkit and Theis maintain that these mechanisms implemented by the federal courts appear to adversely affect the plight of prisoners seeking to file a petition for habeas corpus in the federal courts. Therefore, an erosion of habeas corpus may occur in the future.

Civil Rights of Institutionalized Persons Act

The Civil Rights of Institutionalized Persons Act addresses egregious, or flagrant, conditions in violations of rights, privileges, or immunities given under the Constitution, or laws pursuant to a pattern of practices of deprivation. Those who are sued under this type of litigation are state officials -- custodians. These claims are filed in federal courts. Prisoners typically ask for injunctions or equitable relief. Despite the availability of these five types of legal remedies, inmates are more likely to file civil rights (Section 1983) and habeas corpus claims.

Key Terms

action
assaults
attorney fees
battery
breach
Civil Rights Act
Civil Rights of Institutionalized Persons Act
clearly established
color of law
compensatory damages
damage

defamation
deliberate indifference
failure to train
false imprisonment
"good faith" exception
great writ
habeas corpus action
illegal separation
injunctions
injunctive relief
injury
intentional torts
legal duty
libel
negligence tort
nominal damages
preponderance of the evidence
Prison Litigation Reform Act of 1995
punitive damages
relief in habeas corpus
Romes's Twelve Tables
Section 1983
strict liability tort
supervisory liability
tort
writ of habeas corpus

CASE CITED

Bivens v. Six Unknown Agents of the Federal Bureau of Narcotics (1971)

REFERENCES

Cheurprakobkit, S., and Theis, J. (1999). The decline of habeas corpus. *The Justice Professional.* 12(1):3-16.

Cripe, C. A. (1997). Legal Aspects of Corrections Management. Maryland: Aspen Publication.

The Prison Litigation Reform Act of 1995.

Title VII of the U.S. Code, Section 1983: Civil Action of Deprivation of Civil Rights.

CHAPTER 5

Preventing Inmate Litigation

FOCAL POINTS

- Preventing Inmate Litigation
- Negative Effects of Judicial Intervention
- Positive Effects of Judicial Intervention
- Training Correctional Officers
- Keeping a Written Policy
- Defenses Administrators Can Invoke
- Key Terms

One type of litigation that penal administrators could face is having to comply to a **consent decree** from a court that discovers problems that need to be corrected. Consent decrees are agreements that are entered into (by prison administrators and lawyers and approved by the courts) for the purpose of taking steps to improve conditions in jails or prisons. They have far reaching impact that could last for extended periods of time. Though consent decrees are looked upon favorably by inmates (because they could mean favorable changes to the conditions of prisoners' confinement), they mean something completely different to prison officials and state legislatures. Critics argue that the changes recommended by consent decrees could literally cost an institution hundreds of millions to make, and prisons do not have reserves of money in their budgets. These same critics ask, by what right do prison officials have to enter into agreement to make reforms when they lack the authority to appropriate the needed funds to make changes? Furthermore, critics contend that the monies prisons will use to make corrective action will come from legislative appropriations, or the governor in some cases, but the underlining fact is that the funding that it takes to correct prison problems must be given over long periods of time. This ultimately creates problems because state legislatures might take exception to appropriating strained state budgets to allocate taxpayers resources to populations of prisoners. State legislatures contend that the money could be better used for state transportation, education, medical care, and a host of social programs that are needed by its law-abiding citizens. Despite this, other litigations could come from individual prisoners.

Administrators, guards, medical personnel, and correctional staff can become the targets of lawsuits. Section 1983 and other civil lawsuits are pervasive and can be financially draining on state correctional systems, as well as individuals. However much officials dislike it, inmate litigation is a reality that will probably never disappear. Therefore, correctional administrators must protect themselves from potential lawsuits. One viable approach to defend against inmate litigation is to engage in preventive strategies that will eliminate, or substantially reduce, the likelihood that prisoners will succeed in court. If the court is allowed to intervene, it could make a number of changes such as the following:

A. Place the prison system under the supervision of a special master, monitor, or receiver.

B. Cite prison administrators for contempt for failure to comply with court orders for reform.

C. Prohibit new admissions to prison, causing jails to be clogged up.

D. Order parole boards to release inmates before they have served their complete sentence.

E. Order the prison system to adopt community-based programs, such as work furloughs or weekend releases, to decongest the prison.

F. Encourage the plaintiff and defendant to work out a plan for court approval in the form of a consent decree.

Some Negative Effects of Judicial Intervention in Prison:

A. Create antagonism for the judiciary from the public, the legislature, and prison administrators. Prison administrators, in particular, object to court administration (as opposed to more supervision) of prisons.

and prison administrators. Prison administrators, in particular, object to court administration (as opposed to more supervision) of prisons.

B. The potential to create false expectations among prisoners about major changes in prison conditions could lead to disenchantment since prison reforms do not come easy.

C. Possible loss of control by prison personnel, resulting in more prison violence.

D. Demoralization among prison personnel before morale goes back up again -- if prison reforms work.

E. Diversion of state funds to prisons, which could otherwise have been used for other state projects, such as schools, social work, etc.

Some Positive Effects of Judicial Intervention in Prisons:

A. In general, judicial intervention has improved prison conditions. Prisons are now more humane than they ever were.

B. More money appropriated for prisons from the legislature, which prison administrators could not otherwise have obtained.

C. More attention given by the public, including the mass media, to prisons.

D. Reduction of abuses and lessening of arbitrary decisions involving prisoners.

E. Greater accountability on the part of prison officials, and less secrecy in prison operations.

Cripe (1997) provides strategies that correctional officers can use to reduce being sued. These include (a) teaching correctional employees to follow policies and instructions of their supervisors; (b) creating sound correctional policies, where none exist in places of confinement; (c) employing legal experts to review policies to ensure that they are consistent with constitutional requirements; (d) make sure that correctional policies mirror the most recent Supreme Court decisions; and (e) make sure that there are written policies regarding correctional practices and procedures. These strategies could be very helpful in court.

Teaching Correctional Employees Policy and Following The Instructions of Their Supervisor

Correctional institutions must provide effective training to their employees. The failure to train could be the basis of a lawsuit, signaling to judges and juries with the power to decide cases in favor of inmates that correctional administrations are deliberately indifferent to the plight of those they control. Because the law changes and inmate law constantly evolves, training should be viewed as an ongoing process designed to make officers more effective in executing their duties and contributing to the smooth functioning of the facility.

Creating Sound Correctional Policy

Sound correctional policies are those that are consistent with the recent decisions made by federal courts and the U.S. Supreme Court concerning aspects of corrections. Prison administrators must be abreast of new developments and emerging issues in places of confinement. An omission on the part of the administrator could mean that a constitutionally-sensitive issue might go unaddressed, which could open the door to inmate litigation. Supervisors must be aware of constitutionally-mandated actions and instruct employees to perform their duties with expertise in a manner within the scope of law or risk being sued.

Having A Legal Consultant to Review Correctional Policy

If correctional administrators lack a legal background (to ensure that they are acting within the scope of the law), they should employ legal experts to review their policies to make sure that such policies do not violate the **constitutional rights** of inmates. Moreover, the rights of line officers and staff members must also be safeguarded. The advantage of engaging in legal review could yield quick and easy detection before implementation of policy. Such a practice could later be entered into as evidence that the penal administration was acting in "good faith" if such policies are challenged by inmates.

Correctional Policy Must Mirror Supreme Courts Decision

All correctional policies should mirror, or be consistent with, the decisions handed-down by the Supreme Court where correctional law is concerned. Furthermore, correctional employees should be familiar with the laws that directly affect their job. For example, correctional guards should have knowledge of security, health care, education, and personnel matters. Workers should study how the law affects their agency. They should be knowledgeable about current court rulings on inmates' rights and staff responsibilities. When employees are taught their responsibilities, supervisors should keep records that indicate that employees were trained in the area and the level of competence measured from testing them after training.

Keeping A Written Policy

It is important that agencies keep written policies or procedures on correctional operations. Agencies should keep a record of each person who has been trained and in which areas employees were trained. More importantly, any altercation between inmates and staff should be made a matter of record in case of later civil litigation. In court, these policies could determine who will prevail. If there is a policy in place, it could be instrumental in providing factual information to a judge or jury deciding a case. Having a record is more reliable than solely relying on memory to reconstruct past events.

Another strategy that could help reduce inmate litigation is to create an inmate grievance system. Most prisons today have these systems in place. Allowing inmates to record and submit their grievances to the prison administration could prove to be in the best interest of the facility. Cripe (1997) argues that such practice could have a practical, as well as legal utility. This system allows inmates to report complaints and concerns with procedures and policies affecting all aspects of their treatment in these total institutions. Experts contend that it is good to have this system in place for inmates, because it signals that an administration is receptive towards knowing what inmates think about their treatment. Though **complaints** may not always be decided in their favor, inmates will take some comfort in knowing that they have an avenue to voice their concerns.

A grievance system (a) allows inmates to file a complaint, (b) sets time limits on when a complaint can be filed, (c) requires a description of the action, and (d) must be willing to act with expedience on some claims of inmates, especially those concerning medical issues; physical injuries or the lost of property. A penal administration still has to convince and assure inmates that participation in the program will not bring reprisal. Furthermore, an appeal process should be part of the grievance system. Some noted benefits of this system are that it (a) informs staff of institutional problems, (b) indicates what prisoners regard as major concerns, (c) identifies problem officers who are brutal and harass inmates, (d) serves as a go-between and mediator between two or more inmates that are in conflict, (e) may reduce inmate lawsuits, (f) provides a record for lawyers representing the prison, and to courts giving an account of the facts surrounding a complaint, and (g) provides the agencies an opportunity to correct internal problems that may resort in inmate litigation. Even inmate grievance systems are not without criticisms. For example, the biggest criticism is that they do not provide a remedy that pays damages, and instead focus on corrective measures to eliminate problems. Critics complain that serious problems (disciplinary and malpractice) are not always addressed and that inmates always try to undermine the efforts of such systems by flooding them with large numbers of frivolous complaints. Another impediment of the system is that it sometimes takes extended periods of time to have matters resolved, leading some inmates to view the grievance program as more symbolic, rather than an effective mechanism for redress. Cripe (1997) reports that courts view grievance programs as a very good mechanism to have in place because they reduce the number of lawsuits filed, since trivial or frivolous suits never reach the court. In those instances where cases are filed in court, having a record of the complaint quickly allows judicial officials to resolve the matter at issue. Today, courts require that an inmate's complaint pass through a grievance system, or exhaust other administrative alternatives, before an inmate can file a lawsuit (see Chapter Four).

DEFENSES CORRECTIONAL ADMINISTRATORS CAN INVOKE

The Supreme Court has recognized that the public's interest is served when government officials are able to exercise discretionary duties without fear of litigation. Immunity, absolute or qualified, is a "trade-off," since a person harmed by the actions of a government official may have only damages as a remedy. Officials are human; therefore the possibility exists that they will from time to time make mistakes. On the other hand, some officials may deliberately violate the constitutional rights of others. Immunity is given for the purpose of balancing the public's interest of protecting government officials against the interests of persons injured by acts of officials.

Absolute Immunity

Absolute immunity is reserved for those governmental officials for whom the public's interest requires that they operate free from fear of retaliatory lawsuits and the burdens imposed by being in litigation. Absolute immunity is given to judges and other judicial officials as they discharge the duties associated with their office. Absolute immunity is exclusive to their office; it will not extend to personal activities. For example, if a judge finds a defendant guilty of a crime and sentences him to a term of imprisonment, and the defendant is later cleared, the judge who imposed the sentence cannot be sued because he enjoys absolute immunity. Absolute immunity means that government officials cannot be held personally liable for their decisions.

Qualified Immunity

Qualified immunity extends to other government officials who engage in conduct that does not violate a clearly established constitutional right of which a reasonable person would be aware. This defense is usually invoked when an official claims that a law that he has been alleged to have violated was not clearly established. If the government official knew or should have known that he was violating an inmate's constitutional right, he cannot use qualified immunity as a defense. As such, qualified immunity cannot be used if a government official's actions were guided by malicious intent or mean spiritedness. This defense is designed to protect well-intentioned government officials from facing retaliatory lawsuits, not those who deliberately intended to harm those under their control.

Good Faith Exception

The "good faith" defense creates an exception of liability when it can be established that officials operated in reasonable good faith to adhere to prison regulations and constitutional protection. Prison officials using this defense will probably prevail if they can demonstrate with a show of current policy and record that they actually acted in a manner consistent with their institutional policies. This show of acting in good faith can signal to judges and juries that administrators were not deliberately indifferent to the plight of inmates. If this cannot be established in court, it may be decided that the prison official acted in "bad faith."

Key Terms

absolute immunity
consent decree
good faith defense
qualified immunity

REFERENCE

Cripe, C. A. (1997). Legal Aspects of Corrections Management. Maryland: Aspen Publication.

CHAPTER 6

Inmates and the First Amendment

FOCAL POINTS

- The First Amendment
- Freedom to Receive and Send Mail
- Freedom of the Press
- Freedom of Religion
- Access to Court
- Rights to Association and Visitation
- Some Pertinent Cases
- Key Terms

Amendment I to the United States Constitution states:

> Congress shall make no laws respecting an establishment of religion or prohibiting the free exercise thereof or abridging the freedom of speech, or of the press, or the right of the people peaceably to assemble; and to petition the Government for a redress of grievance.

Under the First Amendment, prisoners can and do bring a variety of claims against correctional institutions alleging a violation of this constitutional safeguard. For example, First Amendment claims typically include freedom to receive and send mail, freedom of the press, freedom of religion, **access to court**, and rights to association and visitation.

Freedom to Receive and Send Mail

The First Amendment to the U.S. Constitution contains the phrase, "Congress shall make no law abridging the freedom of speech." While some have argued that this was exclusive to Congress or the federal government, *Rankin v. McPherson* (1987) maintains that this provision of the First Amendment applies to states, as well as the federal government through the extension of the due process clause of the Fourteenth Amendment. Legal scholars argue that this is logical, since freedom of speech is of the highest concern, and is therefore worthy of the highest degree of protection. Some also argue that of all the amendments in the Bill of Rights, the First Amendment is considered one of the "preferred" amendments because America was founded under a democracy where all citizens have a voice in government. Therefore, it is considered a very important constitutionally-protected liberty.

Of the amendments, the First Amendment is viewed as the most fundamental, and the American court system has treated it as such. However, both state and federal courts have struggled with how such a cherished and fundamental protection would be extended to people in places of confinement (Cripe, 1997). As mentioned earlier, prior to the 1960s, the courts basically ignored the requests of inmates to entertain complaints with correctional institutions and practices. However, *Copper* opened the door to the federal court system for all constitutional violations. *Copper* changed the long standing practice of inaction and opened the door to a flood of litigation of inmates challenging the conditions of their confinement. Chief among their concerns were issues regarding First Amendment violations, such as sending and receiving mail, practicing religion, and accessing the press.

Inmates bringing claims against correctional institutions over their First Amendment right to send and receive mail argue that they have a right to personal and social correspondence with other inmates, family, and friends in the free community. Inmates claim the First Amendment grants them the right to communicate with whomever they choose. Prison officials contend that prison facilities are not like the free community, and serious restrictions must be placed on the communication that inmates have with respect to sending and receiving mail from other inmates, as well as friends and family. Prison administrations argue that it is necessary to place limitations and restrictions on the correspondence of prisoners because of their concerns over (a) the flow of **contraband**, such as drugs, (b) letters that are designed to thwart security, (c) inflammatory correspondence that could encourage racial, religious, gang, or sexual attacks, (d) communication critical of administrators, (e) letters that detail plans of criminal activities upon inmates' release, and (f) letters planning attacks against governmental officials. Because of these concerns, prison facilities require that certain types of correspondence must be censored and checked. If outgoing or incoming correspondence violates institutional policy, the inmates will either not receive incoming mail or be disciplined for trying to send out contraband.

Freedom of Religion

While the First Amendment states that Congress shall make no law respecting an establishment of religion, the incorporation of the Fourteenth Amendment makes this prohibition applicable to the states. The First Amendment clause is also considered a "preferred" amendment, which is given the utmost protection. It provides two rights in cases of religion. First, the **establishment clause** prohibits "an establishment of religion." The clause prohibits the government from creating a national religion. The courts have used the clause to prevent citizens from being forced into certain religious practices. For example, the Supreme Court's ban on mandatory prayers sponsored by public schools is based on the establishment clause of the First Amendment (Smith, 2000). The clause also prohibits the government from funding religious programs. A violation of an inmate's First Amendment rights would occur if a warden of a particular religious faith required that all inmates worshiped the same as he or she, or not worship at all. Likewise, a violation occurs if he or she refuses to allow inmates to worship the religion of their choice when such choice does not create an undue burden or pose a threat to the security, safety, and order of the correctional environment. Second, the free exercise clause states that the government cannot prohibit the free exercise of religious practices. Although this certainly holds true for those in the free community, prison administrators are given leeway because prisons must place, above other concerns, order and security. Thus, they are allowed to create schedules for example, when inmates can engage in worship. This presents a difficult task for prison officials, since prisons are places where different religions are practiced. Many of the religions that are found in prisons are legitimate, others are personal philosophies. Sometimes when inmates feel that their freedom to freely exercise their faith has been denied them, they bring challenges before the court. The courts recognize this task that confronts prison officials and allows great discretion in determining when inmates can engage in the practice of their religion. Cases regarding the practice of an inmate's religion were first addressed in the 1950s and 60s with the emergence of the Black Muslims within the inmate population. Many prison officials resisted recognizing and allowing the establishment of Islam as a faith in places of confinement, while recognizing only traditional Christian religions. They were very suspicious of Islam as a religion, because the Black Muslims were very active in political and social protests occurring in the free community. In fact, they were seen as violent and even thought of as gangs. As a result, inmates practicing Islam were denied opportunities to (a) hold religious services, (b) gain access to religious literature and ministers, and (c) observe religious customs, such as growing beards and special diets that are dictated by their faith. The Muslims claimed that they were denied their First Amendment's right to the free exercise of their religious beliefs and were also denied the Fourteenth Amendment right to equal protection under the law, since Christian inmates were provided the opportunities to hold service, read religious literature, and have a Christian minister. Black Muslims argued that this constituted unequal treatment and therefore sought a remedy. Eventually, the equal protection challenge would be addressed in a case involving a Buddhist prisoner.

Right to Association and Visitation

Though not explicitly stated in the Constitution, inmates are allowed the right of association and visitation. The right of association contains two parts. First, inmates enjoy the right to enter and maintain certain intimate and human relationships (visitation). Second, they have a right to engage in expressive association or gather for peaceful assembly (allowed membership in groups). The latter right is implicitly stated in the First Amendment's guarantee of freedom of speech and to petition the government for a redress of grievances. There are different types of visitations. They range from contact to noncontact to **conjugal visits**. Some argue that allowing visitation makes for good mental health among incarcerated populations, especially where spouse, children, and family members and friends are concerned. If these relationships are healthy, they could add to the successful rehabilitation of offenders or give them something positive to look forward to upon release.

There have also been lawsuits filed over visitation. These suits usually come from two sources. First, attorneys, religious ministers, and court officials may file these suits. Second, family members and friends may also file suits. Visitation by attorneys and religious officials cannot be prohibited, because such would deny prisoners access to the courts and violate their right to freedom of religion. However, visitation hours can be regulated in the best interests of prison order and security (del Carmen, 1991). However, the Supreme Court has not decided if prisoners have a Constitutional right to visitation. There have been a number of cases that the courts have examined with respect to the right to association and visitation.

Freedom of the Press

The First Amendment addresses the right to freedom of the press.

Essentially, it allows the press the right to report what it deems to be newsworthy. However, controversy occurs when reporters and persons associated with the news media contend that the Constitution grants them the right to enter places of confinement and interview prisoners about their experiences and to report and film the conditions of their confinement. Several lawsuits have been filed by persons associated with the media and prisoners seeking to allow the media to exercise their First Amendment right. The courts have consistently argued that in places of confinement, the press or media does not enjoy any First Amendment freedom that exceeds that of any citizen. Therefore, they are not afforded special rights to interview prisoners. The courts have agreed with prison administrations, concluding that such interviews of inmates could create hostility and violence in places of confinement, since those inmates who are interviewed might rise to the status of inmate celebrity.

Access to Court

The First Amendment provides that the people have the Constitutional right to petition the government for a redress of grievance. This provision implies that inmates in jails and prisoners must be afforded the opportunity to bring claims before the judiciary (free from reprisal) if they have grounds or standing to initiate a complaint. All complaints must involve a violation of a constitutional or federal guarantee. For example, if inmates believe that they are subjected to any violation found in the first ten amendments or the Fourteenth Amendment, the complaint is to be taken seriously, especially if the complaint at issue is over one of the preferred amendments. A series of cases have been decided by the courts and the Supreme Court to determine what accommodations must be made by prison officials to ensure that this constitutional protection is not infringed. The Court has said that prison officials must provide inmates with legal assistance and those materials that are necessary to initiate a proper complaint. Almost all correctional facilities in the country have taken this to mean that they must also provide inmates with a law library to keep them abreast of new cases and decisions made by federal courts, as well as the Supreme Court.

Some Pertinent Cases

Bell v. Wolfish
Benjamin v. Caughlin
Block v. Rutherford
Brown v. Johnson
Bounds v. Smith
Cromwell v. Coughlin

Cruz v. Beto
Fulwood v. Clemmer
Garrett v. Estelle
Giano v. Senkowski
Gittlemacker v. Prosse
Goring v. Aaron
Houchins v. KQED, Inc,
Johnson v. Avery
Jones v. Bradley
Jones v. North Carolina Prisoners' Labor Union, Inc.
Kahane v. Carlson
Kentucky Department of Corrections v. Thompson
Lewis v. Casey
Lyon v. Gilligan
Mary of Oakknull v. Coughlin
McCorkle v. Johnson
Moore v. Carlson
Moskowitz v. Wilkinson
Murray v. Giarratano
O'Lone v. Estate of Shabazz
Pell v. Procunier
Pollock v. Marshall
Procunier v. Martinez
Procunier v. Navarette
Rankin v. McPherson
Robert v. U.S. Jaycees
Saxbe v. Washington Post
Smith v. Coughlin
Theriault v. Carlson
Theriault v. Silber
Thongvanh v. Thalacker
Thornburgh v. Abbott
Turner v. Safley
Udey v. Kastner

Fulwood v. Clemmer, 206 F. Supp. 370 (D.D.C.) (1962)

In *Fulwood*, the U.S. District Court of the District of Columbia ruled that the Black Muslim faith must be recognized as a religion and officials may not restrict members from holding services. In this case, the court found that the Black Muslim faith believes in the existence of a supreme being controlling the destiny of man. Therefore, it passes the test as being a legitimate religion. The court did not accept the view of the commissioner of corrections that the Muslims were a "clear and present danger."

Johnson v. Avery, 393 U.S. 483 (1969)

In *Avery*, the Court declared that unless the state provided some effective means for helping illiterate or poorly educated prisoners for post-release conviction relief, it could not prohibit the use of jail house lawyers by inmates in need of legal assistance. To deny such a practice without providing an alternative would essentially violate the prisoners' First Amendment right to court access by denying those prisoners who could not prepare the documents themselves. In *Avery*, the Court enumerated alternative services adopted in other states: (1) a public defender system that supplied trained attorneys paid for by public funds, (2) employing senior law students to interview and advise inmates, and (3) volunteer programs whereby members of the local state bar make periodic visits to prisons and consult with prisoners concerning their cases. In essence, *Avery* suggests that it is very difficult for prisons to prohibit writ writers from practicing their craft, but correctional institutions can place regulations on what they do if it poses a threat to the interests of prison order and security.

Gittlemacker v. Prosse, 428 F.2d (3rd Cir. 1970)

In *Gittlemacker*, the inmate alleged that the officials denied Jewish inmates a full-time rabbi, although they provided Catholic and Protestant chaplains. The response of the prison superintendent was: "The small number of inmates at Dallas, usually two or three, makes the use of a full-time rabbi economically unfeasible and unwarranted." The court also found that the superintendent had attempted to secure services of a rabbi for Jewish inmates. It was asserted that the prison official intended to have him come to the institution on a fee basis. The court rejected the claim by the inmate and concluded that religious discrimination was effectively and conclusively refuted. The court ruled that the state must give inmates the opportunity to practice their religion but is not required to provide a member of the clergy.

Cruz v. Beto, 405 U.S. 319 (1972)

The Court held that if Cruz was a Buddhist and if he had been denied a reasonable opportunity to practice his faith comparable to opportunities afforded to other inmates who practiced conventional religions, the state had discriminated impermissibly against the Buddhist religion. This did not mean, however, that each religious sect, no matter how small, was entitled to identical facilities or personnel. It was sufficient that reasonable opportunities be afforded by the First and Fourteenth Amendments without fear of penalty.

Goring v. Aaron, 350 F. Supp. 1 (D. Minn. 1972)

In *Goring*, a Native American inmate claimed that he made a religious vow at his father's funeral that he would return to old traditions and would not cut his hair. He was punished for refusing to have his hair cut. The federal district court ruled that he could be required to cut his hair while confined, even if cutting it was a religious claim.

Theriault v. Carlson, 339 F. Supp. 375 (N.D. Ga. 1973)

The Church of the New Song, founded by a prisoner, sought to hold services and engage in other practices. The federal court ruled that the First Amendment does not protect so-called religions that tend to mock established institutions and are obvious shams, that tend to mock other established religions, and whose members lack religious sincerity.

Lyon v. Gilligan, 382 F. Supp 198 (N.D. Ohio, 1974)

In *Lyon*, inmates and their wives filed a Section 1983 claim alleging that they were being denied their constitutional rights of privacy, and that such a denial was cruel and unusual punishment. The court ruled that the absence of conjugal visits was not excessive punishment but only a condition of confinement. Moreover, the court asserted that there can be no claim that authorities were denying them access to bedroom activities, which constituted an invasion of privacy because no constitutional violation occurred.

Pell v. Procunier, 417 U.S. 817 (1974)

In *Pell*, the Court argued that a state regulation that prohibits face-to-face interviews did not violate the prisoners' First Amendment rights. The Court reasoned that other methods of communication with the news media existed, such as using mail to communicate directly with inmates, as well as being able to communicate indirectly with journalists through family members, friends, attorneys, clergymen, and others who are allowed to visit inmates. The Court also reasoned that these alternative methods could be used to communicate the conditions of confinement. Moreover, the media could contact former inmates to discuss conditions of their confinement and the treatment they endured.

Procunier v. Martinez, 416 U.S. 396 (1974)

In *Procunier*, the Court found the mail censorship regulations invalid because they restricted inmates' correspondence far more than what was necessary to protect government interests unrelated to the suppression of freedom of speech. Furthermore, the Court found that the prison mail regulations also restricted the First Amendment rights of persons who corresponded with inmates, since they could neither write nor read certain letters freely. However, if, after implementing a less restrictive mail censorship regulation, a letter is still rejected, the inmate involved had to be notified of the rejection. The author of the letter had to be given an opportunity to protest the decision before a prison official not concerned with the original decision. The Court agreed with the District Court in that the bar against using law students and para-professionals for attorney-client interviews could deprive indigent inmates of legal assistance, since some lawyers would hesitate to represent those inmates who could not pay.

Saxbe v. Washington Post, 417 U.S. 843 (1974)

The Federal Bureau of Prisons justified a ban on individual interviews based on what is called the "**Big Wheel Theory**." In this case, the media was not allowed to interview inmates face-to-face because penal administrators argued that such practice created internal problems, since inmates as a result to being interviewed by the media become notorious and are resented by other inmates. In *Saxbe,* the Supreme Court argued the First Amendment does not guarantee to the press a constitutional right of special access to information not available to the general public. In this cases, the Court stated that since the news media were given access to information available to the general public, no violation of the First Amendment occurred. *Saxbe* provided support to prison security and good order. *Saxbe* and *Pell* were decided the same day.

Kahane v. Carlson, 527 F.2d 592 (2d Cir.) (1975)

The court brushed aside objections that special food preparation would be extremely burdensome and expensive for prison authorities, saying that this problem would be surmountable in few of the small number of practicing Orthodox Jews in federal prison. The problem for correctional personnel has been trying to establish who is an Orthodox practicing member of the faith and who is insincere. In *Kahane*, the court argued that most judges would require the provisions of a diet sufficient to sustain the prisoner in good health without violating the Jewish dietary laws. The case decided that Orthodox Jewish inmates have the right to a diet consistent with their religious beliefs unless the government can show cause why it cannot be provided.

Theriault v. Silber, 331 F. Supp 578 (W.D. Tex. 1975)

Theriault and other inmates created a religion called Church of the New Song (CONS) that only allowed inmates as members. They wrote scriptures and demanded group meetings and other activities. CONS requested a paid leader or chaplain as other groups in prison enjoyed. However, members of CONS requested, as part of their religious practice in a special ceremony, to have steak (filet mignon) and wine (sherry). The federal court in Northern Georgia stated that while CONS had an entitlement to the free exercise of their religion, the request for steak and wine went too far, and was therefore denied. Though this case occurred in Georgia, CONS in Texas was found to be masquerading as a religion and was viewed as nothing more than prisoners attempting to disrupt the orderly flow of the Texas Department of Corrections. It was not deemed as being entitled to the First Amendment protection.

Bounds v. Smith, 430 U.S. 817 (1977)

In *Bounds,* state prisoners in North Carolina brought a lawsuit in federal court claiming that the prison system denied them reasonable access to court which was established in *Avery*. The prisoners contended that the prison system was in violation of their First and Fourteenth Amendment rights. The Court argued that prisoners have a constitutional entitlement to access the courts and that protecting that right requires prison authorities to assist inmates in the preparation and filing of "meaningful legal papers" by providing adequate law libraries for the prisoners' use or legal assistance from persons trained in the law. The Court also listed alternatives that prisons can use to provide access to court which include (1) training inmates as paralegal assistants to work under lawyers, (2) using para-professionals and law students as volunteers, (3) hiring lawyers on a part-time basis, and (4) organizing volunteer attorneys and lawyers from other groups to assist prisoners. This decision is an extension of *Avery* and reaffirms the constitutional rights of prisoners to access the courts.

Garrett v. Estelle, 536 F.2d 1274 (5th Cir. 1977)

Garrett, a news reporter, asked to film the first execution to take place in Texas under its new capital punishment statute. In this case, the question was raised whether the media had the right to film and televise executions. Garrett's request was denied (pursuant to a Texas statute). The Court of Appeals of the Fifth Circuit citing *Pell* ruled that the First Amendment does not require the news media to have access to matters that are not accessible to the general public. The state argued that televising executions would be tantamount to reinstating public executions.

Jones v. North Carolina Prisoners' Labor Union, Inc., 433 U.S. 119 (1977)

In *Jones*, inmates filed a Section 1983 suit challenging a statewide regulation that prevented them from joining the prison union. They claimed that the regulation infringed upon their First and Fourteenth Amendment rights. A district court agreed, stating that the regulation was unconstitutional. The case was appealed to the Supreme Court. The Court held that the prisoners' First Amendment rights had not been infringed upon by the ban on membership, solicitation, and group meetings, since inmates do not have those first amendment rights that are inconsistent with their prison status or with legitimate objectives of the corrections system. Moreover, the Court argued that restrictions imposed by prison authorities on union activities were reasonable and consistent with legitimate operational considerations of the institution. In this case, the prison union membership had grown very large. The union advocated better working conditions, higher wages, and better working hours for prisons. In essence, the union wanted to engage in collective bargaining with prison officials. As a result of its relative power, the union was banned by prison officials in the state correctional system. The prisoners claimed a violation of the equal protection clause because groups such as AA, Jaycees, and the Boy Scouts of America were not banned from the prison system. The Court stated that these groups were seen as providing a rehabilitative function to prisoners and these organizations were desired in prison. The Court also said that prison officials do not have to treat all inmate groups alike. In the final analysis, the Court stated that associational rights may be curtailed whenever prison officials reasonably conclude that such associations could disrupt prison order and security.

Moskowitz v. Wilkinson, 432 F. Supp. 947 (D. Conn. 1977)

In *Moskowitz*, an Orthodox Jewish inmate at the Danbury Federal Correctional Institution filed suit when authorities ordered him to remove his beard, which he had grown based on his religious teachings. The prison asserted that its interest in requiring no beards was based on a need to maintain security. Officials argued that growing beards made it difficult to recognize and identify prisoners. In this case, the court argued that the "**no beard rule**" was an impermissible infringement on the inmate's sincerely held religious beliefs, and that punishing him for refusing to shave his beard was unconstitutional.

Houchins v. KQED, Inc., 438 U.S. 1 (1978)

The Supreme Court reviewed an attack by a TV station on a refusal of a sheriff to allow journalists to visit and photograph a portion of the county jail where a prisoner had committed suicide and where conditions were very poor. In *Houchins*, the Court established that the media does not have any more rights than the general public to access jails and other government institutions. Therefore, such institutions need not grant the press extra privileges. The Court relied on *Saxbe* and *Pell.*

Moore v. Carlson, Civil No. 77-982, (M.D. Pa. 1978)

In *Moore*, a Rastafarian inmate claimed that he must allow his hair to grow under the teachings of that religion. However, prison officials argued that the dread locks posed a security problem because the hair prevented a complete search. The officials thought that contraband could be secreted in the hair. The court agreed that the hair must be cut for purposes of institutional security.

Procunier v. Navarette, 434 U.S. 555 (1978)

State prison officials enjoy qualified immunity from an inmate's Section 1983 action alleging interference with his outgoing mail unless (1) the officials knew or reasonably should have known that their actions would violate the inmate's constitutional rights, or (2) the officials acted with malicious intent to cause a constitutional right violation. (In this case,

Navarette filed a claim concerning mail that was not sent out in 1972. *Procunier v. Martinez* was decided in 1974). The fact that in 1972 clearly established First and Fourteenth Amendments rights did not exist with respect to correspondence of inmate mail precludes the contention that the officials knew or should have known that their actions would violate a constitutional right. The Court argued in this case that negligence alone will not support a claim for damages in federal court under Section 1983.

Bell v. Wolfish, 441 U.S. 520 (1979)

In this case, the Court articulates that "double bunking," the "publishers only rule," body cavity searches of pretrial detainees after contact visits, and searching of a pretrial detainee's quarters in his absence are constitutional. It also examined a challenge to a Federal Bureau of Prisons regulation that required inmates to receive hardback publications from the publishers only. The "publishers only rule" was implemented because of concerns of contraband being smuggled into the correctional facility. The Bureau of Prisons justified this restriction on the grounds of security concerns. Prison officials argued that books and magazines were hard to examine throughly for contraband, and by limiting the sender to the publishers only, it was thought that the threat of contraband would be minimized. The Bureau of Prisons amended it policy to allow paperback books and magazines to be sent by family and friends. However, hardbacks were still restricted to the publishers only.

Block v. Rutherford, 468 U.S. 576 (1984)

In *Block*, a group of detainees brought a claim under Section 1983 challenging a sheriff's policy that allowed only contact visits by pretrial detainees with spouses, relatives, and friends. The district court agreed, claiming that denying inmates the right to embrace spouses and family created an impermissible burden on the detainees. The district court also asserted that the policy was punitive and had an exaggerated security concern. The Supreme Court reversed citing the standard established in *Bell v. Wolfish.* The Court held that a non-punitive ban on contact visits for pretrial detainees based on legitimate fears for institutional security does not violate the Fourteenth Amendment provisions. In *Block*, the Court said that the policy was related to legitimate governmental objectives. *Wolfish* concluded that there is no reason to believe that pretrial detainees pose any lesser security risk than convicted inmates.

Jones v. Bradley, 590 F.2d 294 (9th Cir. 1979)

An inmate at the Washington State Penitentiary asked to use the chapel and to perform marriages, claiming he was a pastor of the Universal Life Church (ULC). The district court dismissed his complaint, holding that the ULC is not a religion and not entitled to First Amendment protections. The court of appeal held it was improper to inquire into the "truth" of religious beliefs or to discredit them because of their unusual nature. The court decided that it was a religion and was entitled to some First Amendment protection. However, the court objected to empowering the group with the ability to perform marriages because that was a matter regulated by state licensing commission and not a free exercise protection.

Brown v. Johnson, 743 F.2d 405 (6th Cir. 1984)

In *Brown*, prison officials placed a ban on the Metropolitan Community Church (MCC) services and activities because the church preached to the needs of a homosexual congregation. Officials testified about the strong correlation between inmates' homosexuality and prison violence. They also argued that to allow worship services would essentially increase the risk of violent confrontation by identifying homosexuals in the prison population. The court agreed with the prison, citing safety and orderly needs as a reason to uphold the regulation.

Mary of Oakknull v. Coughlin, 475 N.Y.S. 644 (N.4. App. Div. 1984)

Inmates brought a Section 1983 action claiming that the prison conjugal visitation program was limited to those prisoners who could show a valid marriage certificate to verify their married status before they could participate in the program. The court upheld the program's restrictions and noted that there is no constitutional right to conjugal visits. Moreover, the court stated that the standard for visitation of any type is to be determined by prison officials based on their experience and judgement.

Robert v. U.S. Jaycees, 464 U.S. 609 (1984)

In this case, the Court said that there are two types of freedom of association protected by the Constitution. The first is the right to enter into and maintain human relationships. This implies that a right exists to have family relationships and the need for (privacy) protecting it. The Court stated that prisoners forfeit this right because of the conditions of incarceration. However, an exception might be in cases where "conjugal visits" are allowed. The second type of right to association is "expressive association." This is the right to gather with others to take part in activities that are specifically protected by the First Amendment: the right to speak, worship, and petition the government for a redress of grievances.

Smith v. Coughlin, 748 F.2d 783 (1984)

In *Smith*, the Second Circuit Court of Appeals upheld New York's restriction on visits to death row inmates, which limited visitation to family members only and did not allow visits with friends and acquaintances. *Smith* placed limits on associational rights. The court of appeals stated in this case that the visitation policy was based on security and administrative concerns. These concerns justified the policy, thereby making it constitutional.

Udey v. Kastner, 805 F. 2d (5th Cir.) (1986)

In this case, the request of an inmate of unknown religious origin to have a special diet based on religious interpretation of certain biblical text was denied by the court. The inmate requested only organically grown produce, which was to be washed in distilled water. A lower court held that meeting the request of the inmate's diet would create an undue burden on the prison system. In *Udey*, the appeals court argued that granting this request would only lead to a probable proliferation of claims for special food.

O'Lone v. Estate of Shabazz, 41 Cr.L. 3251 (1987)

In a 5 to 4 majority, the Court applied the standard it had just enunciated one week earlier in the *Turner* case to a prisoner's suit based on the First Amendment's Free Exercise clause. In *Shabazz*, Muslim inmates at a New Jersey prison brought challenge against two prison regulations, one of which prevented them from engaging in the weekly exercise of their religious practice, Jumu'ah. Because of security concerns and demands on staff time, prison officials prohibited inmates who were working outside at work details from coming back inside the prison during the day, except for emergencies. This prevented the Muslims on the outside from attending Jumu'ah services. In this case, despite the court of appeals' reversal of the district court opinion stating that the free exercise rights of the prisoners had been violated without the state showing whether some method of accommodation could be achieved, the Supreme Court disagreed, stating that the appeals court should have respected and deferred to the judgement of prison officials. Relying on *Turner*, the majority decided that the policies were reasonably related to legitimate penological interests.

Turner v. Safley, 41 Cr.L. 3239 (1987)

In a 5 to 4 decision, the Supreme Court said that the proper standard for assessing whether or not a prison regulation violates inmates' constitutional rights is not "strict scrutiny," but rather whether or not the rule bears a reasonable relationship to legitimate penological interests. The majority set out four factors bearing on the reasonableness determination and then applied this test to uphold a Missouri prison regulation restricting inmate-to-inmate mail. However, the Court struck down another prison regulation that severely limited inmate marriages. In *Turner*, the Court stated that a prison regulation that impinges upon inmates' constitutional rights is valid if it is reasonably related to legitimate penological interests.

Pollock v. Marshall, 845 F. 2d 656 (6th Cir. 1988)

Inmate Pollock claimed that his religious beliefs in the Lakota America Indians taught him that hair was sacred and should not be cut. Marshall, the Superintendent, argued that Pollock was not a true believer because he was not born a Lakota Indian and he could not become one by professing to accept the faith. The court assumed that Pollock did believe in the religion of the Lakota Indians and applied the Turner test. The Sixth Circuit Court of Appeals found that the prison regulation had a legitimate purpose in controlling the flow of contraband, and controlling security was a compelling state interest that justified the ban on long hair.

Benjamin v. Coughlin, 708 F. Supp. 570 (S.D.N.Y.) (1989)

In *Benjamin*, Rastafarian inmates requested a special diet based on their religious teachings. The diet involved no meats but foods raised only with organic fertilizers and cooked in natural materials, such as clay pots. The court in this case ruled that prison authorities did not have to supply these food items because they were too complex and providing them would present too heavy a financial and administrative burden.

Kentucky Department of Corrections v. Thompson, 490 U.S. 454, 109 S.Ct. 1904 (1989)

Inmates at the State Penitentiary at Eddyville, Kentucky, brought a class action under Section 1983 challenging the enforcement of Kentucky's regulation that excluded certain prison visitors. The Supreme Court ruled that prison officials were not required to provide a hearing before terminating the visiting privileges of persons who were deemed to pose a threat to institutional security or the orderly running of the visiting room.

McCorkle v. Johnson, 881 F.2d 993 (11th Cir. 1989)

Inmate McCorkle filed a Section 1983 claim asserting that authorities were violating his constitutional rights by restricting the exercise of his Satanic religion. The court of appeals affirmed a district court ruling that officials had not violated the inmate's First Amendment rights. The state argued that Satanism is not a religion and that McCorkle was not a true believer in the religion. The court ruled that policy was valid in prohibiting McCorkle from practicing his religion. The court stated that the policy was justified in maintaining security and order and was therefore reasonably related to a legitimate penological concern. This case was not difficult to decide because McCorkle had stated that part of his religious belief included making human sacrifices and eating human flesh.

Murray v. Giarratano, 109 S.Ct. 2765 (1989)

In *Giarratano*, a death row inmate brought a Section 1983 claim against the Virginia Department of Corrections and its director, Edward W. Murray, for failing to provide him with counsel at the state's expense to pursue collateral proceedings or post-conviction relief. Giarratano maintained that his Sixth (right to a trial) and Fourteenth Amendment (due process and equal protection) rights were violated. In this case, the Court relied on *Pennsylvania v. Finley* (1986), where it ruled that the Constitution does not require states to provide counsel in post-conviction proceedings. This ruling, the Court contended, applies to capital, as well as noncapital offenses. The Court ruled that neither the due process clause of the Fourteenth Amendment nor the equal protection guarantee of "meaningful access" required that the state appoint counsel for indigent prisoners seeking post-conviction relief. In this case, the Court also cited that even *Gideon v. Wainwright* (1963) established that the right to a lawyer only extended to the trial stage and the initial appeal from the judgement and sentence of the trial court. The Court also remarked that although a death row inmate is not entitled to a Constitutional appointment to have a lawyer at the state's expense in post-conviction proceedings, most state and federal law provide a lawyer in these cases.

Thornburgh v. Abbott, 490 U.S. 401 (1989)

In *Thornburgh,* inmates and some publishers filed a class action suit against a prison regulation. The prison followed the Federal Bureau of Prisons regulation that allowed inmates to receive publications from outside the prison. However, officials could reject material they thought were detrimental to security, good order, or discipline of the institution, or if it might facilitate criminal activity. The regulation listed several types of prohibited publications that threaten institutional security, including materials on how to make drugs, how to use weapons, those that encourage violence, and certain sexually explicit materials (those that involved children). The lawsuit challenged the prison regulation citing it as a violation of the First Amendment. The Supreme Court identified that inmates and publishers have a First Amendment interest in receiving and sending the contested publications. First, the Court addressed the question of what standard of review should be applied to these First Amendment rights. The Court decided on *Turner* instead of *Procunier v. Martinez* asserting that *Procunier* was too limited in its analysis and application. The Court held that prison regulations regarding receipt of publications by inmates are valid if reasonably related to a legitimate penological interest. By using *Turner*, the Federal Bureau of Prisons' regulation was found not to be exaggerated and was permissible because there was no obvious alternative that could have achieved the same result.

Cromwell v. Coughlin, 773 F. Supp. 606 (S.D.N.Y 1991)

In *Cromwell*, a federal court agreed that the Commissioner of Corrections in New York has the discretion to allow prison visitation programs in general and who can participate in conjugal visitation programs in particular.

Thongvanh v. Thalacker, 17 F.3d. 256 (1994)

Thongvanh, an inmate, brought a Section 1983 action against an Iowa prison, alleging a violation of his First (free speech) and Fourteenth Amendment (due process and equal protection under the law) rights . At trial, a jury agreed that there were violations of his constitutional rights and awarded him $4,000. The court of appeals affirmed the judgement. The court argued that the Iowa prison had legitimate prison concerns when it inspected all mail and was within the scope of the law by requiring that all correspondence be in English only. However, the courts criticized the prison for not explaining or showing why correspondence in Lao could not be translated, and then checked to see if Thongvanh had violated the rules based on the content of his correspondence to his family members who were not English speaking. This was of concern to the court, especially since there was a refugee service center that provided translation to the Iowa Reformatory. The court also noticed that though the prison policy on inmate correspondence specified an English only mail policy, there were exceptions made for Spanish-and-German speaking inmates. This constituted a violation of the Fourteenth Amendment's Equal Protection Clause. The appeals court in this case used *Turner v. Safely*.

Giano v. Senkowski, 54 F.3rd. 1050 (2d Cir. 1995)

An inmate (Giano), brought a Section 1983 lawsuit claiming a violation of his First Amendment right to receive correspondence. Giano challenged a policy at the Clinton Correctional Facility at New York that prohibits inmates from receiving nude and semi-nude photos of spouses and girlfriends. Officials at Clinton allowed inmates to receive other erotic literature and publications such as *Playboy Magazine*, but argued that the restriction of the nude and semi-nude photos was necessary in order to prevent violent confrontations if such photos were somehow possessed by other inmates. Prison officials argued that because of the possibility of those confrontations, there was a threat to the security, safety, and good order of the institution. In the case, the Second Circuit Court said that this action and policy did not violate Giano's First Amendment right. The court concluded that the policy was based on a valid and rational concern about maintaining prison order and security.

Lewis v. Casey, 64 L.W. 4587 (1996)

Casey and other prisoners in the Arizona State Department of Corrections brought a class action suit against officials in Arizona, alleging a violation of the First, Sixth, and Fourteenth Amendments. Inmates claimed that the Department of Corrections deprived them of their rights to access the courts and counsel through inadequate legal research facilities. Inmates claimed that such practices are direct violations of *Bounds* (this case held that the right to access to court requires that prison authorities assist inmates to prepare and file meaningful legal papers by providing them with adequate law libraries or adequate assistance from persons trained in the law). In deciding this case, the Court argued that what the inmates failed to show was widespread actual injury they sustained from what they believed constituted inadequate facilities. The inmates did not demonstrate that the alleged shortcomings in the library or legal assistance program actually hindered their efforts to prepare a legal claim. The Court argued that though the law libraries or legal assistance programs were found to be insufficient, this was not enough to establish a violation of the right to access the court. The Court took its opinion a step further by stating that *Bounds v. Smith* had been misinterpreted to mean that inmates have a right to a law library or legal assistance. Instead, *Bounds* merely acknowledges a right to access the court. This case essentially gives correctional administrations the right to remove or discontinue the many expensive law libraries in correctional settings around the country as long as they still allow inmates access to courts.

Key Terms

establishment clause
First Amendment Clause
free exercise clause

CASES CITED

Fulwood v. Clemmer, 206 F. Supp. 370 (D.D.C.) (1962)
Johnson v. Avery, 393 U.S. 483 (1969)
Gittlemacker v. Prosse, 428 F.2d (3rd Cir. 1970)
Cruz v. Beto, 405 U.S. 319 (1972)
Goring v. Aaron, 350 F. Supp. 1 (D. Minn. 1972)
Theriault v. Carlson, 339 F. Supp 375 (N.D. Ga. 1973)
Lyon v. Gilligan, 382 F. Supp. 198 (ND, Ohio, 1974)
Pell v. Procunier, 417 U.S. 817 (1974)
Procunier v. Martinez, 416 U.S. 396 (1974)
Saxbe v. Washington Post, 417 U.S. 843 (1974)
Kahane v. Carlson, 527 F.2d 592 (2d Cir.) (1975)
Theriault v. Silber, 391 F. Supp. 578 (W.D. Tex. 1975)
Bounds v. Smith, 430 U.S. 817 (1977)
Garrett v. Estelle, 536 F.2d 1274 (5th Cir. 1977)
Jones v. North Carolina Prisoners' Labor Union, Inc., 433 U.S. 119 (1977)
Moskowitz v. Wilkinson, 432 F. Supp. 947 (D. Conn. 1977)
Houchins v. KQED, Inc., 438 U.S. 1 (1978)
Moore v. Carlson, Civil No. 77-982, Pa., 1978

Procunier v. Navarette, 434 U.S. 555 (1978)
Bell v. Wolfish, 441 U.S. 520 (1979)
Jones v. Bradley, 590 F.2d 294 (9th Cir. 1979)
Block v. Rutherford, 468 U.S. 576 (1984)
Brown v. Johnson, 743 F.2d 405 (6th Cir. 1984)
Mary of Oakknull v. Coughlin, 475 N.Y.S. 644 (N.4. App. Div. 1984)
Robert v. US Jaycees, 464 U.S. 609 (1984)
Smith v. Coughlin, 748 F.2d 783 (1984)
Udey v. Kastner, 805 F.2d (5th Cir. 1986)
O'Lone v. Estate of Shabazz, 41 Cr.L. 3251 (1987)
Rankin v. McPherson, 483 U.S. 378 (1987)
Turner v. Safley, 41 Cr.L. 3239 (1987)
Pollock v. Marshall, 845 F. 2d 656 (6th Cir. 1988)
Benjamin v. Caughlin, 708 F. Supp 570 (S.D. N.Y.) (1989)
Kentucky Department of Corrections v. Thompson, 490 U.S. 454, 109 S.Ct. 1904 (1989)
McCorkle v. Johnson, 881 F.2d (11th Cir. 1989)
Murray v. Giarratano, 109 S.Ct. 2765 (1989)
Thornburgh v. Abbott, 490 U.S. 401 (1989)
Cromwell v. Coughlin, 773 F. Supp. 606 (S.D.N.Y 1991)
Thongvanh v. Thalacker 17F. 3d. 256 (1994)
Giano v. Senkowski, 54 F. 3rd 1050 (2d Cir. 1995)
Lewis v. Casey, 64 L.W. 4587 (1996)

REFERENCES

Cripe, C. A. (1977). Legal Aspects of Corrections Management. Maryland: Aspen Publications.

del Carmen, R. V. (1991). Civil Liabilities in American Policing: A Text for Law Enforcement Personnel. Englewood Cliffs, NJ: Brady Press.

Smith, C. E. (2000). Law and Contemporary Corrections. Belmont, CA: West/Wadsworth Publishing Company.

CHAPTER 7

Inmates and the Fourth Amendment

FOCAL POINTS

- The Fourteenth Amendment
- Discussion of Searches and Seizures
- Some Pertinent Cases
- Key Terms

Amendment IV to the United States Constitution states:

> The right of the people to be secure in their persons, houses, papers, and effects against unreasonable searches and seizures, shall not be violated and no warrants shall issue but upon probable cause, supported by oath or affirmation and particularly describing the place to be searched, and the persons or things to be seized.

Prisons and jails are places used to incapacitate or warehouse, offenders who have committed crimes, been found guilty, and sentenced by a court of law. They are confined because they have preyed on people in society and pose a threat to the community. While confined, these inmates do not quickly abandon old habits and are capable of demonstrating the same behavior they committed in the free community. The evidence of their criminal history reveals that they are capable of committing the most heinous types of behavior against fellow inmates, correctional guards, and prison officials, if the opportunity presents itself. Therefore, one of the responsibilities of those charged with keeping watch over inmates is to ensure that the correctional environment is free and safe from the flow of contraband that could include drugs and weapons. Drugs can counteract any rehabilitative potential that an offender might receive while confined, and a weapon could be used to assault, or otherwise kill, another person. Subsequently, these items pose a serious threat to the safety, security, and order of places of confinement.

The Fourth Amendment does not prevent searches and seizures, but rather protects against unreasonable searches and seizures. Though one can understand why this challenge may be raised by someone in the free community claiming that overzealous police officers violated his or her constitutional right by not following proper procedure, the question becomes a stretch when one imagines prisoners making the same assertion of having protections against searches and seizures within the confines of their living quarters. The job for courts has been twofold. First, they must ask, is the area of the search protected under the Constitution? Second, if so, has the search been conducted in a reasonable manner? The Supreme Court has said that inmates have no Constitutional protection from cell searches. This means that when prison officials believe that an inmate is secreting contraband, a weapon, or stolen property, the inmate's cell and belongings can be searched without a court-issued warrant and without due process. Furthermore, an inmate's living quarters may include a cell, room, or dormitory. Searches are also extended to other areas within the prison, such as work and recreational areas, as well as grounds surrounding the building. Searches are an essential practice, because they can reveal contraband, escape plans, or weapons that could be used to cause the death of someone.

The Fourth Amendment opinions of the Supreme Court illustrate the difficulty of balancing the right to privacy of the inmates with the needs of prison institutions to prevent the flow of contraband and to promote security and safety. The Courts have routinely decided with the rights of prison officials to promote the smooth function of prison operations. There are different types of searches that can be conducted in places of confinement that range from a stop and frisk (a pat down for safety reasons) to body cavity searches, urine testing, X-rays, and blood tests. The latter two will be discussed later.

Some searches are not so intrusive, yet others can be very intrusive. While acknowledging this, the Court has indicated that any search and seizure must be reasonably based on a legitimate justification by prison officials. Moreover, the method of the search cannot be unnecessarily excessive. For example, the Court has stated that inmates could attach the Eighth Amendment claim of cruel and unusual punishment to the Fourth Amendment claim if prison guards are abusive (amounting to harassment) in the searching methods. del Carmen (1991) contends that two questions must be asked by an officer before conducting a search of an inmate. First, does the inmate have a reasonable expectation of privacy in the area, or part of his person, that is to be the target of the search? Second, is the search reasonable? The Supreme Court has said of cell searches that the reasonableness of a search is assessed by (1) the scope of the intrusion, (2) the manner in which the search is conducted, (3) the justification for initiating the search, and (4) the place where the search is conducted.

The most commonly used type of search almost always targets the inmate's cell. This is the rule. This type of search does not involve a search of the inmate's person. Strip or body cavity searches are the exception. The courts have been careful not to allow the ordinary search of a cell to turn into a fishing expedition. Because body cavity searches are intrusive, the only time that they are justified is when the inmate is suspected of having contraband, especially drugs secreted on his person. Body cavity searches have been harder for administrators to justify than cell searches. The opportunities that present such risks occur after inmates return from unsupervised visits, contact visits, participating in work release, and court appearances. Anytime an inmate is allowed to leave a place of confinement or have access to or contact with others in the free community, the possibility exists that he can smuggle contraband into a correctional facility. This alone may warrant a strip and body cavity search. Although a body cavity search is intrusive, the courts have found them to be valid if they are justified and conducted properly so as not to humiliate the prisoner. As long as these searches can be viewed as part of a policy clearly related to an identifiable and legitimate institutional need and not intended to humiliate or degrade, they will be upheld as valid practices. The Court has said that these searches must be conducted in a professional manner, in private, away from other inmates and correctional guards who are not a part of the search team. For example, if an inmate is made to strip in the presence of other inmates and guards, the experience would be very humiliating and could lead to violence perpetrated on the examining guards and inmates who are onlookers by the inmate who is the object of the search. The Court has said that these searches must be done calmly and as matter-of-factly as possible (Cripe, 1997).

Inmates cannot be routinely strip searched without a valid reason. The only actions that justify strip searches is a belief that an inmate has contraband or that he may have a weapon kept on his person. These actions necessitate a strip or body cavity search, because they pose a threat to the order, security, and safety of inmates, guards, and prison officials.

Another interesting area that the Fourth Amendment covers is the search of persons (spouses, friends, and family members) who visit prisons and jails. To what extent can prisons and jails subject visitors to searches? The Court has stated that if reason exists to believe that a visitor is bringing contraband to an inmate, the person may be subjected to a search or pat down. The visitor can also be subjected to a body cavity search, but prison officials would do well to procure a warrant before engaging in such practices. Male or female visitors can be subjected to a plain or body cavity search at the request of a prison guard, because he or she believes that the visitor is smuggling contraband. These searches may also be conducted by gender-specific officers. These searches are acceptable as long as the guards do not fondle the genitals or anus of the visitors. The Supreme Court has had to resolve such issues. The Court has stated that correctional facilities must have a stated policy indicating that a search could be made of all visitors. The policy should be visible for all visitors and the search must be justified based on a reasonable suspicion that the visitor has contraband. However, reasonable suspicion is not necessary to search visitors because of the threat of the flow of contraband.

Correctional guards are not exempted from being searched. They, too, can be searched if there is reasonable suspicion that they are involved in smuggling contraband. When suspicion surfaces about a correctional officer, it is usually corroborated by reliable inmates or other guards who have witnessed such behavior in the past. When an employee is subjected to a search, it may include a search of an officer's locker, clothes, wallet, or even his person. Prison officials would do well to first get a search warrant from a local judge before performing searches of employees. This may indicate that they acted in good faith by first having probable cause to believe that an officer was smuggling contraband into the facility.

Some Pertinent Cases

Bell v. Wolfish
Block v. Rutherford
Dunn v. White
Forts v. Ward
Goff v. Nix
Hudson v. Palmer
Jordan v. Gardner
Lanza v. New York
Lee v. Downs
Stone v. Powell
United States v. Hearst
United States v. Hitchcock
Watson v. Jones

Lanza v. New York, 370 U.S. 139 (1962)

Inmate Lanza had a visit from his brother in a local jail. The two talked in the visiting room. Unknown to them was an electronic device in the room that picked up their conversation, and a transcript was made of their conversation. A state legislative committee investigating corruption in the state parole system called Lanza to testify based on the content of the transcript of the conversation. Lanza refused to testify and was convicted based on his refusal. He alleged that it was improper for jail officials to electronically record his visitation room conversation. He contended that his Fourth Amendment protections were violated, and that he was punished for refusing to talk about the contents of an intercepted conversation. The Supreme Court disagreed and upheld the conviction stating that a jail is not the equivalent of a house or car, where there might be a reasonable expectation of privacy. A jail is not a constitutionally protected area.

Goff v. Nix, 803 F.2d 358 (8th Cir. 1968)

In this case, inmates at the Iowa State Penitentiary complained and brought a Section 1983 challenge of the policy requiring that inmates be subjected to a strip search before and after visitation, even if the visitor was a lawyer or religious leader. Moreover, inmates were also strip searched if they went to court, received medical attention, or visited recreational areas in the prison. In *Goff*, the District Court banned strip searches, that occurred after an inmate received a visit from his lawyer and after receiving medical attention. The District Court argued that to subject inmates to a strip search after visits from their lawyer or after receiving medical attention would serve to discourage them from participating in these constitutionally-protected areas. The Court of Appeal reversed and upheld the policy of strip searches, maintaining that inmates could smuggle contraband in body cavities if these searches were not conducted. Despite this decision, the Appeals Court argued that while strip searchers are done, officers cannot use "rude and offensive" language, because such is verbally harassing and demeaning to inmates. This type of practice bears no relationship to the prison's need to conduct the searches.

United States v. Hitchcock, 467 F.2d 1107 (1972)

In this case, the prisoner claimed that documents kept in his cell were protected from admission into evidence, because his cell afforded him a reasonable expectation of privacy. The Ninth Circuit Court of Appeals disagreed contending that a cell does not share any attributes of privacy such as a house, automobile, or hotel. Therefore, the court ruled that a warrantless search of a cell is not unreasonable, and documentary evidence found as a result is not subject to suppression. It is not reasonable to expect a prison cell to be accorded the same level of privacy as a home, automobile, or hotel.

Stone v. Powell, 428 U.S. 465 (1976)

In this case, two state prisoners sought release from prison in a habeas corpus case filed in federal district court. One inmate was convicted of murder in state court, in part, on the basis of testimony concerning a pistol taken from him when he was arrested for violating a vagrancy ordinance. The prisoner sought the exclusion of the evidence during trial in a state court, alleging that the ordinance was unconstitutional, hence the arrest was invalid. The other inmate was also convicted of murder in state court based in part on evidence seized pursuant to a warrant that the inmate claimed was invalid. In this case, the Court said that a habeas corpus petition in federal court will not be granted based on an alleged violation of the Fourth Amendment right if the same allegation was raised and rejected earlier in state court during the criminal trial.

United States v. Hearst, 563 F.2d 1331 (9th Cir. 1977)

In *Hearst*, a court of appeal upheld a conviction over an objection that it was obtained using evidence of an intercepted conversation Hearst had in jail. While in San Mateo County Jail in California, she had a visit from a friend. They communicated by phone through a glass partition. The conversation was monitored and recorded by jail staff. The taped conversation was given to the FBI and later used against Hearst at trial. Hearst argued that the tape should not be admitted as evidence because it violated her Fourth Amendment right. The court ruled that jail officials had a justifiable security purpose in monitoring and recording conversations of inmates with their visitors. Moreover, once the government established a justifiable purpose for its intrusion on the individual's rights, the question of the constitutionality of the jail's actions was to be resolved in its favor. The court cited the Supreme Court's decision in *Procunier v. Martinez*.

Bell v. Wolfish, 441 U.S. 520 (1979)

In their first decision involving the rights of pretrial detainees, as opposed to prisoners convicted after trial, the Court ruled that such practices of housing two inmates in rooms designed for one, conducting inmate body searches after visits, and forbidding the receipt of most hardbound books could all be justified as reasonably related to the goals of security and smooth jail administration. However, on a practical level, the important part of the *Bell v. Wolfish* opinion may prove to be the majority's criticism of lower federal court judges for allowing themselves to become "enmeshed in the minutiae of prison operations"-- a signal that the Supreme Court is not happy with the burgeoning field of prisoner's rights litigation. In this case, the Court articulated that "double bunking," the "publishers only rule," body cavity searches of pretrial detainees after contact visits, and searches of a pretrial detainee's quarters in his absence are constitutional.

Forts v. Ward, 621 F.2d 1210 (2d Cir. 1980)

In *Forts*, female inmates at the Bedford Hills Correctional Facility in New York brought a class action suit under Section 1983 challenging a correctional policy that assigned male guards to duty in the female sleeping quarters. The suit maintained that such a practice was a violation of the females' right to privacy under the Fourth Amendment, because male officers could see them either partially or completely nude. Prison officials contended that to deny male officers the opportunity to work in the sleeping quarters of women would constitute a violation of Title VII of the Civil Rights Law and disadvantage male officers. In *Forts*, the Court of Appeals was faced with the task of balancing the interests of the female inmates' right to privacy and the employment rights of the male guards. The Court of Appeals struck a balance by having the women's sleeping quarters provided with curtains so that they could shield themselves from the view of male guards while sleeping. They were also provided with appropriate sleep wear. The Appeals Court reasoned that the privacy protection covered only the involuntary viewing in prison of parts of the body by male officers and did not extend to a protection against being viewed at all while asleep.

Lee v. Downs, 641 F.2d 1117 (4th Cir. 1981)

In *Lee*, the court ruled that where a female prisoner was possibly suicidal, it was proper for correctional officers to forcibly remove her clothes in the presence of male officers. However, the court ordered that staff members may not supervise inmates of the opposite gender in toilet and shower areas, whether or not this rule is inconvenient to the administration.

Block v. Rutherford, 468 U.S. 576 (1984)

Pretrial detainees at the Los Angeles County Central Jail brought a class action under Section 1983 against the County Sheriff, certain administrators, and county board supervisors. Inmates complained of shake down searches that occurred while inmates were away at recreation, meals, or other activities. The detainees argue that not being present at the time of cell searches deprived them of their liberty interest without due process of law in violation of the Fourth and Fourteenth Amendment. In *Block*, the Court ruled that because jail officials have a legitimate concern about the flow of contraband in the facility (detainees are no less threatening than convicted inmates), the practice that they use that does not allow inmates to be present is upheld because such a practice is reasonably related to a legitimate governmental objective. Moreover, the Court stated that detainees do not have a constitutional right to contact visits or to observe shakedowns. In *Block*, the Court reiterated its decision in *Bell v. Wolfish.*

Hudson v. Palmer, 35 Cr.L. 3230 (1984)

Palmer, an inmate at the Bland Correctional Center in Virginia, was serving sentences for forgery, grand larceny, and bank robbery convictions. Hudson, an officer at the Correctional Center, conducted a shakedown search of Palmer's prison locker and cell with another officer. The officer discovered a ripped pillow case in the trash basket near his bunk. Palmer was charged with destroying state property. He was found guilty at a prison disciplinary hearing and was ordered to reimburse the state for the cost of the pillow case. In addition, a reprimand was entered on Palmer's prison record. Palmer brought a Section 1983 lawsuit claiming that Hudson brought false charges against him and conducted the search of his cell to harass him. The Court in this case stated that the Fourth Amendment right against unreasonable search and seizure affords an inmate absolutely no protection from searches and seizures in his cell. Officials may search cells without a warrant and seize materials found there. The Court also stated that the Eighth Amendment provision against cruel and unusual punishment could, however, provide an inmate a way to challenge harassment tactics by prison guards.

Dunn v. White, 45 Cr.L. 2360 (1989)

Inmate Dunn objected to a prison policy requiring all prisoners to take a blood test to identify those infected with AIDS. Dunn argued that such forced testing was a violation of the Fourth Amendment right against unreasonable search and seizure. In Dunn, a court of appeals ruled that drawing Dunn's blood in a prison hospital setting was the equivalent of drawing blood in any hospital setting to determine DUI cases. Therefore, the court ruled that there is no unreasonableness associated with the "seizure of blood," even when an inmate objects to such an intrusion.

Watson v. Jones, 980 F.2d 1165 (8th Cir. 1992)

In *Jones*, two male inmates brought a Section 1983 challenge against a female correctional guard who fondled their genitals and anuses when subjecting them to a strip search. According to the inmates, they were subjected to daily strip searches in which the female guard engaged in "prolonged rubbing and fondling of the genitals and anus areas." The inmates contended that such behavior is a clear violation of their Fourth Amendment right to be free from an unreasonable search. The Circuit Court of Appeals agreed, stating that "sexually harassing and physically intrusive pat-down searches" are unreasonable and go beyond a proper search within the meaning of the Fourth Amendment, because they are too intrusive and are tantamount to sexual harassment.

Jordan v. Gardner, 986 F.2d 1521 (9th Cir. 1993)

In *Jordan*, the Ninth Circuit Court of Appeals held that male officers could not conduct pat searches of female prisoners. In this case, the Court of Appeals discovered that many of the women inmates had been the victims of sexual abuse before being sentenced to prison. Relying on testimony from psychiatrists and psychologists, the court determined that if male officers conducted pat searches of women offenders, the experience would be a traumatic ordeal, since many of inmates had sexual abuse histories prior to being sentenced to prison. Moreover, the court indicated that to allow pat searches of women with a history of sexual abuse could be seen as subjecting them to cruel and unusual punishment.

Key Terms

habeas corpus petition
vagrancy ordinance

CASES CITED

Lanza v. New York, 370 U.S. 139 (1962)
Goff v. Nix, 803 F.2d 358 (8th Cir. 1968)
United States v. Hitchcock, 467 F.2d 1107 (1972)
Stone v. Powell, 428 U.S. 465 (1976)
United States v. Hearst, 563 F.2d 1331 (9th Cir. 1977)
Bell v. Wolfish, 441 U.S. 520 (1979)
Forts v. Ward, 621 F.2d 1210 (2d Cir. 1980)
Lee v. Downs, 641 F.2d 1117 (4th Cir 1981)
Block v. Rutherford, 468 U.S. 576 (1984)
Hudson v. Palmer, 468 U.S. 517 (1984)
Dunn v. White, 45 CrL 2360 (1989)
Watson v. Jones, 980 F. 2d 1165 (8th Cir. 1992)
Jordan v. Gardner, 986 F.2d 1521 (9th Cir. 1993)

REFERENCES

Cripe, C. A. (1997). Legal Aspects of Corrections Management. Gaithersburg, MD: Aspen Publication.

del Carmen, R. V. (1991). Civil Liabilities in American Policing: A Test for Law Enforcement Personnel. Englewood Cliffs, N.J.: Brady Press.

CHAPTER 8

Inmates and the Eighth Amendment

FOCAL POINTS

- The Eighth Amendment
- Discussion of Cruel and Unusual Punishment
- Some Pertinent Cases
- Key Terms

Amendment VIII to the United States Constitution states:

> Excessive bail shall not be required nor excessive force imposed, nor cruel and unusual punishments inflicted.

Though the hands-off approach was a standing practice that lasted into the mid 1960s, it would not be until the 1970s that the federal courts would review cases where prisoners alleged violations of the Eighth Amendment right which prohibits cruel and unusual punishment. The Eighth Amendment has been tied to prisoners' rights and their need for decent treatment and minimal standards of health. Dilulio (1990) argues that by the mid 70s, the federal courts began examining the operations of correctional institutions to determine if they operated within the parameters of the law where the Eighth Amendment was concerned.

The language found in the Eighth Amendment that specifically speaks to the issue of corrections is that punishment should not be imposed in a cruel and unusual manner. Dilulio contends that claims brought by prisoners under this amendment address issues such as (a) harsh sentences, (b) death penalty sentences, (c) conditions on death row, (d) conditions in prisons, (e) medical treatment, (f) violence committed by fellow inmates and guards, and (g) inmate suicides.

Harsh Sentences

Inmates sometimes challenge the constitutionality of their sentences citing that it is a violation of the cruel and unusual punishment clause. Moreover, the Eighth Amendment has been used to provide guidelines for sentences that have been disproportionate to the gravity of the criminality committed by the offender. For example, in 1909, the Court reviewed a case where an offender had received a prison sentence of 12 to 20 years to be served at hard labor. The judge presiding over the case ordered the offender to serve the sentence through the entire period wearing ankle and wrist chains. In this case, the crime that the offender was found guilty of having committed was being an accessory to someone who falsified a government document. On its reversal, the Supreme Court argued that to impose such a sentence on an accused would constitute a violation of the Eighth Amendment prohibition against cruel and unusual punishment, because the sentence was too severe. The Court also stated that when a sentence is imposed in a manner that is disproportionate to the offense committed and exceeds that which is necessary to accomplish a sentencing aim, such behavior is cruel and unusual punishment. In a similar case decided in 1958, the Supreme Court reversed a decision under Martial law that stripped a soldier of his U.S. citizenship for deserting the military during wartime. The Court ruled that such a sentence was too harsh and was a violation of the cruel and unusual punishment clause of the Eighth Amendment. The Court, in this case, stated that the Eighth Amendment must draw its meaning from "evolving standards that mark the progress of a maturing society."

Death Penalty Sentences

The United States Supreme Court has said that the death penalty is constitutionally valid and that it may be an appropriate sentence that expresses the community's beliefs about the consequence that an individual or individuals should face depending on the crime they committed. Despite this statement, the Court has objected to how the death penalty has been imposed on some offenders. In 1972, the Court mainly objected to the "arbitrary and capricious" manner in which it had been imposed. In a landmark case, the Court objected to the imposition of the death penalty by stating that "no meaningful basis exists to distinguish cases in which it was imposed, and in other cases, when it was not imposed." However, four years later the same state (Georgia) revisited the issue. This time, the Court was satisfied with the creation of procedural safeguards that prevented the "wanton and freakish" imposition of the death sentence. In this case, unlike before, juries were instructed to consider aggravating and mitigating circumstances in each case. Furthermore, while establishing the death penalty does not constitute cruel and unusual punishment when it is imposed in a proper manner, the Court has rejected the imposition of this sentence in instances where some state prisons have mandated an automatic death sentence on prisoners who engage in murder while serving a sentence of life without the possibility of parole. The Court has also rejected the imposition of the death penalty in states where it has been mandated for all offenders who engaged in first degree murder, in cases where juries found that aggravating circumstances outweighed mitigating circumstances, or where offenders had committed the act of rape. The Court has stated such cases do not meet "civilized standards" that mark "contemporary values."

Conditions of Death Row

Inmates have sought to challenge the conditions of their confinement on death row as being cruel and unusual punishment. They contend that because they are placed in segregation (separated from the general population), eat and receive medical attention in their cell, and spend near twenty- hours each day in their cell, these conditions alone are cruel and unusual and, are therefore, in violation of the Eighth Amendment. In a recent case, the Supreme Court has refused to rule on a complaint brought by a death row inmate who contends that being on the "row" for seventeen years is a violation of the Eighth Amendment. The Court has indicated that the matter should first be addressed by the lower courts before it rules on such a matter. Yet, the Court has said that prisoners on death row cannot be held in "barbarous and torturous" conditions, because such a practice is not consistent with standards of decency that mark an evolving society. However, death row inmates can be segregated from other inmates in the general population who are serving a regular sentence, some of whom will be eligible for parole. In a similar case, an inmate on death row challenged the conditions on the "row" by complaining of being subjected to poor ventilation, unsanitary food and bedding, use of inmates as prison guards, a lack of physical exercise, and inadequate plumbing. He argued that these conditions constituted cruel and unusual punishment. The Court dismissed all but the complaint of the deprivation of physical exercise. The Court said that because inmates on death row are locked down for nearly twenty-hours each day, providing them exercise is a necessity.

Conditions in Prison

Inmates have filed claims alleging that the conditions of their confinement violate the Eighth Amendment right to be free from cruel and unusual punishment. Courts have stated that while an inmate is expected to serve his sentence of imprisonment, the experience of imprisonment should not be predicated on punishment in and of itself. Inmates have argued that such matters as overcrowding (leading to tension between inmates and facilitates violence) and double bunking are unconstitutional. In the first such case addressed by the Court in 1967, it ruled that a civilized standard of human decency does not permit a man, for a substantial period of time, to be exposed to and deprived of the basic elements of life. The Eighth Amendment forbids inhuman treatment that violates concepts of decency. Recently, the Court has used the "totality of circumstances" standard to determine if prison conditions are, in fact, cruel and unusual. This can be established if a prison official can be shown to be "deliberately indifferent" to the needs and circumstances of prisoners.

Prison overcrowding has been a hot issue for inmates who charge that it constitutes cruel and unusual punishment. Inmates claim that because of overcrowding, they must share cells with other inmates and that crowds of inmates create conditions that are unsanitary and conducive to violence and inhumanities. The Court has not completely agreed with this assertion from inmates. The Court, however, has stated that prison overcrowding alone does not in and of itself constitute cruel and unusual punishment, but rather the totality of circumstances associated with overcrowding is the basis of cruel and unusual punishment. For example, the Court has stated that if conditions create a "deprivation of basic needs" amounting to the infliction of wanton pain, cruel and unusual punishment exists. When examining issues related to the Eighth Amendment, the courts normally consider the quality and amount of medical and mental health services, the extent of violence, the quality of food, and the availability of recreational opportunities (Adler, Mueller, and Laufer, 1994). However, overcrowding can be cruel and unusual punishment.

Medical Treatment

The Court has stated that prisoners have a right to medical services. The Court argues that since prisoners are in the custody of the state, the state must therefore provide prisoners with that amount of medical treatment, which is comparable to that available to the general public. Cripe (1997) argues that because the government has incarcerated people, inmates are not able to receive ordinary sources of health care that they might receive were they in the free community. This is the case, even if prisoners have contracted tuberculosis, the AIDS virus, suffer from a mental condition, or refuse treatment. Although the Court has been sympathetic to the medical needs of prisoners, it has not intervened much with respect to individual complaints of negligence or inadequate treatment. However, in cases where it finds the entire medical delivery system in a prison to be substandard and in violation of adequate health care, it is more likely to respond. Gilman (1977) contends that when the Supreme Court discovers that an entire health care system suffers in the areas of severe understaffing, unsanitary medical equipment, or learns that contagious inmates are allowed to interact with the general population, thereby posing a threat to others' health, the Court is likely to find this a violation of the Eighth Amendment. The Court has established that in order to raise a claim of inadequate medical treatment under Section 1983, an inmate has to prove that failure to provide treatment or inadequate treatment was shocking, barbaric, willful, or involved deliberate indifference to the request for needed medical attention. The Court has said that dissatisfaction with the quality of medical attention is not enough to effect a cause of action under a Section 1983 claim.

A critical issue facing correctional institutions in America is the concern over the AIDS virus. Prisons and jails are high risk places for the spread of infectious disease. Sennott (1994) contends that the rate of AIDS among prison populations is nearly fourteen times higher than the general population. AIDS has become the leading cause of death among prison inmates (Cauchon, 1995). In 1993, the Centers for Disease Control (CDC) reported 11,565 cases of AIDS in the nation's prisons (Crawford, 1994). Despite this statistic, 3,500 inmates in jails and prisons have died from HIV-related complications. A national survey conducted in 1995 on the number of jail and prison inmates reported to be carriers of AIDS estimates that the figure is nearly 80,000 (see Cauchon, 1995). Surveys also indicate that none of the nation's jails and prisons are immune from this epidemic. This issue has forced prison administrators to ask many questions, some of which include what treatment is to be given to prisoners who are infected with the HIV/AIDS virus. Are prisoners constitutionally entitled to receive AIDS treatment or can they refuse any medical treatment if they desire? Should the quality of AIDS treatment be equivalent to that received by people in the free community? Are HIV/AIDS prisoners to be segregated with similarly situated prisoners or placed within the general population? Do fellow cell mates have the right to know if they share a cell with someone who is HIV positive or has full blown AIDS? Do officers have a right to know which prisoners are affected by the disease so as to take precautionary steps not to become infected? The courts have consistently ruled that these prisoners are entitled to medical treatment. Therefore, correctional administrators must be informed about the current level of medical care and precautionary treatments that are provided in the free community, and try to follow those guidelines. Failure to do so could constitute a show of deliberate indifference to the plight of prisoners.

Violence Committed by Fellow Inmates and Guards

Another aspect of the prohibition of cruel and unusual punishment includes excessive and deadly force perpetrated at the hands of guards and violence from other inmates. Some degree of force might be expected, and even legal, in the prison setting. What is not accepted is the use of excessive and deadly force. When a prison guard engages in the use of excessive or deadly force, his behavior can be a violation under state torts, state penal codes, and the Civil Rights Act. But, how is the level of force to be determined as reasonable? As a general rule, correctional guards are allowed to engage in the amount of force that is not likely to resort in death or serious bodily injury (del Carmen, 1991). Officers, generally, can only engage in the level of force which is considered to be reasonable under the circumstances to which they are confronted. Since circumstances may vary, one can expect that the level of force may differ. Officers would be wise to use only the amount of force necessary to accomplish a specific goal. Stated another way, the amount of force that an officer uses can be determined by the amount of resistance initiated by an inmate. Sometimes reasonable force can quickly escalate into excessive force or deadly force depending on whether an inmate is threatening the life of another prisoner or correctional official. However, the officer must remain cautious in the use of reasonable force to subdue prisoners. Officers must take caution to use force to control the inmate and the correction's environment and not use force to punish the prisoner. Such use of intentional punishment could open the door for legal liabilities. Though inmates can bring claims alleging Eighth Amendment violations, the standard set by the Supreme Court is that the prisoner has the burden of showing that the correctional guard or prison official acted with deliberate indifference. However, in cases where inmates are violently attacked (physically or sexually) by other inmates, the standard shifts from a showing of deliberate indifference to establishing that the prison official "knowingly disregarded an excessive risk of harm" that a reasonable person would have known to have likely occurred. This standard is more difficult to establish.

Though excessive force can be justified, deadly force is governed by state law, departmental policy, and thc Constitution. Officers working for any department of correction must be guided by the department's policy. Nearly all departments have policies on the use of deadly force but limit its use to specific circumstances. Officers are justified in using deadly force in self-defense, in defense of another person, to prevent an inmate's escape, and to control a prison riot (del Carmen, 1991). If the officer deviates from the departmental policy while engaging in the use of deadly force, he is acting outside of the scope of departmental policy and might invite liability. Officers should be familiar with departmental policy on the use of deadly force, and if no policy exists, the officers should follow state law.

Inmate Suicides

Each year, jails and prisons are places that experience a high number of inmate suicides. There are a number of reasons experts give to explain why an inmate would probably engage in this fatal act. Explanations range from inmates suffering from depression or other mental problems to being ashamed or embarrassed over having been a victim of rape or being under the influence of drugs. Experts also argue that suicides typically occur in jails, because they lack a classification system, and as a result, jails contain passive and aggressive inmates and even a large number that might be insane. Because of the pervasive nature of inmate suicide, both jail and prison administrators must do something to prevent such actions from occurring. After inmates are taken into custody and can no longer provide for themselves, custodians must provide for the health and safety needs of inmates.

When inmates commit suicide, surviving families bring suits seeking damages in federal and state court. They usually file a Civil Rights Action or wrongful death action. Plaintiffs charge that custodians are responsible for the inmate's death due to failure to properly convey information on suicide prevention, recognize signs of suicidal symptoms, provide a safe environment, properly train employees, act promptly after suicide, and remove materials that make suicides successful. More specifically, lawsuits charge that custodians failed to prevent the deceased from taking his own life, and the institution's staff should have intervened to prevent the suicide. According to Kappeler, Vaughn, and del Carmen (1991), in some negligent tort cases the actions by jail administrators, or detainees, can create a "special duty" for jailers. They contend that a special duty arises when the detainee's actions give custodians reason to believe he or she could be a threat to himself, herself or others. Moreover, when a detainee demonstrates self-destructive behavior and the inability to take care of himself the way a reasonable person demonstrates, this creates a special duty for custodians to prevent harm.

In a civil rights action, the plaintiff must show that the custodians acted with deliberate indifference. In proving deliberate indifference, a plaintiff must show the defendant knew the deceased was capable of committing suicide and did nothing to prevent it. In civil rights cases, federal courts recognize custodians owe a duty of reasonable care to plaintiffs, and that duty depends on the risk that is reasonably perceived (Collins, 1990). Federal action suits require that the plaintiff show that (1) the defendant acted under the color of law, and (2) the decedent was deprived of a federal protected right. Though these requirements appear easy to prove, Cohen (1992) argues that federal courts are making it difficult, but not impossible, to prove liability requirements.

While Collins (1990) argues civil action suits require the plaintiff to prove that custodians failed to provide "reasonable care" as defined by courts through state statutes under the common law, Kappeler (1993) contends that plaintiffs must establish that a special duty existed and jail administrators breached that duty. If the duty is not established, officers will not be held liable. Kappeler argues that plaintiffs must establish foreseeability by proving that the jailer's breach of preventing the suicide attempt substantially contributed to the suicide. Basically, inmates who have attempted suicide, or the family of the deceased, have to show negligence. Civil actions demand damages. They address issues, such as the negligent loss of property, failure to protect the inmate from harm, medical malpractice, or breaches of duties of reasonable care that correctional staff may owe inmates. Moreover, failure to properly train, supervise, or assign staff are other issues that come under state suits.

Some Pertinent Cases

Blumhagen v. Sabes
City of Revere v. Massachusetts General Hospital
Doe v. Coughlin
Estelle v. Gamble
Farmer v. Brennan
Furman v. Georgia
Gates v. Rowland
Gregg v. Georgia
Harris v. Thigpen
Heflin v. Stewart County
Helling v. McKinney
Hudson v. McMillian
Holt v. Sarver
Hutto v. Finney
Jackson v. Bishop
Jolly v. Coughlin
Logue v. United States
Myers v. Lake County
Reed v. Woodruff County
Rhodes v. Chapman

Roe v. Fauver
Ruiz v. Estelle
Smith v. Wade
Talley v. Stephens
Washington v. Harper
West v. Atkins
Whitley v. Albers
Wilson v. Seiter
Wood v. White

Talley v. Stephens, 247 F. Supp. 683 (E.D. Ark.) (1965)

Talley, an inmate in Arkansas, suffered from discriminatory and brutal treatment, including receiving nine lashes with a leather strap for filing a complaint against prison officials. During this time in the Arkansas prisons, selected prisoners were allowed to supervise other inmates and determine which inmates would be given a whipping, even in some cases giving other inmates whippings. Those inmates allowed to whip others were usually the most violent offenders in the prison. In this case, the Court said that because of the way corporal punishment was administered in the Arkansas Penitentiary, there were no safeguards to prevent widespread abuse. As such, the Court ordered corporal punishment forbidden. Despite this ruling, the court did not say that the Constitution forbids corporal punishment.

Jackson v. Bishop, 404 F.2d 371 (8th Cir. 1068) (1968)

In *Jackson*, the court wanted to create standards and procedures that would prevent arbitrary, discriminatory, and excessively brutal beatings that were still occurring post-*Talley*. In Jackson, the federal court concluded that standards and procedures could not keep abuses from occurring. Officials did not always follow written procedures, and excessively brutal whippings still took place. Inmates were still whipping other inmates, and this posed a threat to security and rehabilitation. The appeals court argued that whippings violated the Eighth Amendment's prohibition against cruel and unusual punishment.

Holt v. Sarver, 300 F. Supp. 825 (E.D. Ark.) (1970)

In *Holt*, a federal court cited the Cummins Farm Unit of the Arkansas State Penitentiary as being in violation of the Eighth Amendment. The court cited the use of inmates as prison guards and said that prisoners had a constitutional right of protection by the state while they were incarcerated. As the judges noted, a system that relies on trustees for security and that houses inmates in barracks, leaving them open to "frequent assaults, murder, rape and homosexual conduct," is unconstitutional.

Furman v. Georgia, 408 U.S. 238 (1972)

In *Furman*, the Court held that the death penalty violates the equal protection clause of the Fourteenth Amendment and the prohibition against cruel and unusual punishment, and is therefore unconstitutional. In this case, the Court put an end to the prior use of the death penalty. The Court found that it was imposed at the complete discretion of the judge or jury, and the practice was in violation of the Eighth Amendment. The Court argued that the practice that Georgia had in place essentially led to the arbitrary and capricious imposition of the death sentence. The Court found "no meaningful basis for distinguishing the few cases in which it was imposed from the many cases of which it was not imposed." The Supreme Court was not satisfied with Georgia's procedure of imposing the death penalty.

Logue v. United States, 412 U.S. 521 (1973)

Inmate Logue was arrested by U.S. Marshals on charges that he had smuggled marijuana into the United States. He was placed in the Nueces County Jail in Texas to await trial. However, while in custody, Logue committed suicide in jail by hanging himself. His surviving family filed a lawsuit against the United States contending it was responsible for the wrongful death of Logue under the Federal Tort Claims Act. In this case, the Supreme Court held that though Logue was placed in jail as a federal prisoner by a Deputy U.S. Marshal, he was under the immediate control of the local sheriff and his staff, and not the U.S. Marshal. According to the Court, liability under the Federal Tort Claims Act requires that any negligent action be committed by a "federal agency." The Nueces County Jail was under contract with the federal government and not a federal agency. The Tort Claims Act had excluded a contractor with the United States from the definition of a federal agency. This protected the United States from liability for the negligent acts, or omissions, of the jail's employees.

Estelle v. Gamble, 429 U.S. 465 (1976)

Inmate Gamble was confined in the Texas Department of Corrections. He was injured at work when a bale of cotton fell on him. When he complained, he was sent to the hospital. From there he was sent to his cell to rest. When he returned to the hospital in increased pain, he was given pain pills. The next day, he saw a doctor who prescribed a pain reliever and a muscle relaxant. He was placed by medical orders on "cell-pass." After a week, the doctor prescribed another pain reliever. Despite continuing pain, the doctor said he could return to light work. When Gamble refused to work, he was taken before a prison disciplinary committee, which ordered him to be seen by another doctor. This second doctor ran tests and prescribed additional medication. Gamble was ordered several times to go to work, but continued to refuse saying that he was in too much pain. He was eventually placed in solitary confinement as a disciplinary sanction for refusing to work. He then claimed chest pains and black outs. He was also seen in the hospital for these problems. When he reported pain to guards in administrative segregation, he was refused permission to see a doctor. Gamble than filed a Section 1983 claim alleging a violation of his Eighth Amendment right to be free from cruel and unusual punishment. The Court held that deliberate indifference to a serious illness or injury constitutes cruel and unusual punishment in violation of the Eighth Amendment. However, evidence showed that Gamble had been seen by medical personnel seventeen times in a three-month span. Failure to make proper diagnosis in this instance would constitute, at most, medical malpractice, but not cruel and unusual punishment. The Court made no decision as to the complaint against the prison warden or the Director of the Department of Corrections, but remanded the case to the Court of Appeals for the Fifth Circuit for consideration of this point. In essence, this case states that since a prisoner cannot secure needed medical care for himself or herself, as one in the free community, institutions have a legal right to provide inmates with adequate medical services.

Gregg v. Georgia, 428 U.S. 153 (1976)

In *Gregg,* the Court reasoned that death penalty statutes containing sufficient safeguards against arbitrary and capricious imposition are constitutional. Gregg found a formula for sentencing under the Eighth and Fourteenth Amendments that was lacking in Furman. The State of Georgia created a requirement that at least one aggravating factor had to be found by a jury to exist beyond a reasonable doubt before a death sentence could be imposed. This satisfied the Court's concern in Furman that the death sentence was imposed in an arbitrary and capricious manner. In addition to the one aggravating factor, a jury in a death penalty case could consider other aggravating and mitigating factors before imposing the death penalty. Georgia also provided an automatic appeal for all death penalty sentences to the Georgia Supreme Court.

Hutto v. Finney, 437 U.S. 678 (1978)

In *Hutto*, the Supreme Court upheld a lower court decision that solitary confinement in the Arkansas prison lasting for more than thirty days constitutes cruel and unusual punishment in violation of the Eighth Amendment. The Court summarized three principles regarding the Eighth Amendment: courts should (1) consider the totality of the conditions of confinement, (2) specify in remedial orders each factor that contributed to the violation and for which a change would be necessary to remove the unconstitutionality, and (3) specify, when appropriate, minimum standards that, if met, would remedy the entire constitutional violation. In this case, the Court indicated that courts should defer to correctional officials and legislators unless they find that conditions are deplorable or sordid.

Bell v. Wolfish, 441 U.S. 520 (1979)

In their first decision involving the rights of pretrial detainees, as opposed to prisoners convicted after trial, the Court ruled that such practices as housing two inmates in rooms designed for one, conducting inmate body searches after visits, and forbidding the receipt of most hardbound books could all be justified as "reasonably related" to the goals of security and smooth jail administration. In this case, the Court articulated that double bunking is constitutional. The Court argued that it is the due process clause of the Constitution and not the Eight Amendment that protects a pretrial detainee from certain conditions and restrictions. The Eighth Amendment deals with punishments, which cannot be cruel and unusual. Because a pretrial detainee has not been convicted, he or she cannot be punished at all; therefore the cruel and unusual punishment clause does not apply.

Ruiz v. Estelle, 503 F. Supp. 1265 S.D. Tex. (1980)

In *Ruiz*, the Texas Department of Corrections (TDC) was cited for permitting grossly deficient and unconstitutional prison conditions. In this case, appellate court judge Justice condemned what had become a familiar litany of deplorable conditions of incarceration: brutality by guards, extreme overcrowding, inadequate medical care, a lack of staff training, disciplinary hearing improprieties, a trustee system that allegedly delegated security functions to inmates, and interference with inmates' access to the courts. In *Ruiz*, the court invoked the appropriate constitutional safeguards of the Eighth and Fourteenth Amendments and looked at the totality of the circumstances occurring at TDC.

Rhodes v. Chapman, 452 U.S. 337 (1981)

The Supreme Court concluded that double ceiling alone does not constitute cruel and unusual punishment. Most of the justices stressed that the lower federal courts had given this particular prison (the Southern Ohio Correctional Facility, a maximum security institution built in the early 1970s) generally high marks. Writing for the majority, Justice Powell stated that prison conditions "must not involve the wanton and unnecessary infliction of pain, nor may they be grossly disproportionate to the severity of the crime warranting imprisonment." Deprivation of basic human needs "could be cruel and unusual, but conditions that are restrictive and even harsh" are not unconstitutional unless they can also be said to violate contemporary standards of decency. "To the extent that such conditions are restrictive and even harsh," Justice Powell wrote, "they are part of the penalty that criminal offenders pay for their offenses against society." In this case, double ceiling was not found to cause deprivations in food services or other essential areas or to have increased the level of violence. The practice did reduce job and educational opportunities, but such deprivations do not rise to the constitutional level. The justices also emphasized that the decision in this case did not mark the end of judicial intervention in prison matters. In *Rhodes*, the Court argues double ceiling of prisoners does not, in itself, constitute cruel and unusual punishment.

City of Revere v. Massachusetts General Hospital, 463 U.S. 239 (1983)

In this case, the court held that government entities must take all reasonable steps to make sure that medical care needs of those in prisons or jail are provided.

Smith v. Wade, 33 Cr.L. 3021 (1983)

Daniel Wade, an inmate, voluntarily checked into a protective custody unit in a reformatory for youthful first-time offenders, because of prior incidents of violence against him. Due to disciplinary violations, he received a short term in punitive segregation before being transferred to administrative segregation. On the first day he was in administrative segregation, he was placed in a cell with another inmate. William Smith, a correctional guard, placed another inmate in the cell with Wade. The third inmate was in administrative segregation for fighting, and Smith never checked to see if another cell was available in which to place the third inmate. Subsequently, Wade was harassed, beaten, and sexually assaulted. He brought action under Section 1983 against the correctional guards and officials, contending that he was subjected to cruel and unusual punishment, which violates his Eighth Amendment rights. Punitive damages may be awarded, in addition to compensatory, damages if a correctional officer acts with reckless or callous disregard of, or indifference to, the rights and safety of inmates.

Whitley v. Albers, 475 U.S. 312 (1986)

A corrections officer was taken hostage and held in a cell on the upper tier of a cellblock during a riot in an Oregon Penitentiary. The prison security manager consulted with two other prison officials and it was agreed that forceful intervention was necessary to protect both the hostage and the non-participating inmates. A squad of officers armed with shotguns entered the cellblock in order to rescue the hostage. One officer was ordered to fire a warning shot and to shoot low at any prisoner climbing the stairs towards the hostage cell. After the rescue squad began moving up the stairs, a warning shot was fired, followed by another shot. A third shot hit the prisoner in the left knee as he was climbing up the stairs. The inmate sustained severe damage to his left leg, as well as mental and emotional distress. As a result, he brought a lawsuit under Section 1983 against prison officials alleging a violation of his Eighth and Fourteenth Amendments. The Court ruled that the shooting of a prisoner without prior verbal warning to suppress a prison riot did not violate the prisoner's right against cruel and unusual punishment. Liability arises only if such deadly force was used with "obduracy and wantonness."

Doe v. Couglin, (D.C.N.Y. No. 88-CV-964) (1988)

In this case, a prisoner diagnosed with the acquired immunodeficiency syndrome (AIDS) was placed in an isolation ward with other AIDS-infected inmates. The unnamed prisoner, Doe, filed a class action suit alleging that his right to medical record confidentiality had been violated as a result of his transfer. In this case, the appeals court agreed with Doe and ordered that his records were confidential. The court ruled that disclosure would subject the inmate to harassment and psychological pressure from other inmates and officials.

Roe v. Fauver, 43 Cr.L. 2174 (1988)

Prisoners with AIDS in New Jersey prisons are barred from mingling with the general prison population. Roe, who had AIDS, was held in solitary confinement. She objected that this confinement constituted a degree of cruel and unusual punishment. However, the appellate court ruled that prison health considerations must take priority over individual comforts, and that although Roe was inconvenienced by the solitary confinement, the prison policy was designed to improve the safety of all prison inmates.

West v. Atkins, 108 S.Ct. 2250 (1988)

Inmate West tore his left Achilles tendon while playing volleyball at a state prison in North Carolina. A physician at the prison transferred West to the Central Prison Hospital in Raleigh for orthopedic consultation. Samuel Atkins, M.D., a private physician, provided orthopedic services at the prison hospital through a contract for professional services. He treated West's injury by placing his leg in a series of casts over several months. West brought a Section 1983 claim alleging that his Eighth Amendment right to be free from cruel and unusual punishment had been violated. West claimed that Atkins knew that he needed surgery but refused to schedule it, eventually discharging him when his ankle was still swollen and painful. West contended that Atkins acted with deliberate indifference towards his medical needs by failing to provide adequate treatment. The Supreme Court agreed, stating that under state law the only medical care that West could receive for his injury was that provided by the state. If Doctor Atkins misused his power by demonstrating deliberate indifference to West's serious medical needs, the resultant deprivation opened the door for litigation. The Court stated that by virtue of West being in state custody, he was owed medical attention, since he could not receive medical attention independent of his custody. The Court said that private physicians who fail to provide adequate medical care when contracted by prisons are "acting under color of law" when treating prisoners.

Wood v. White, 689 F. Supp. 874 (W.D. Wis. 1988)

In *Woods*, the court ruled that an inmate does retain some privacy rights to his medical records, especially where his HIV/AIDS status is at issue, but there are instances where the prison has a legitimate interest in disclosing that information. In this case, instead of creating a new rule about releasing this sensitive information, the court said that each case would have to be examined on an individual basis, whereby the privacy rights of the inmate and the legitimate governmental interests of needing to disclose such information are weighed.

Washington v. Harper, 58 L.W. 4249 (1990)

Inmate Harper was sentenced to prison in 1976 for robbery. From 1976 to 1980, he was incarcerated at the Washington State Penitentiary in the mental health unit. Harper was paroled in 1980. One of the conditions of his parole was that he participate in psychiatric treatment. In December 1981, his parole was revoked after he assaulted two nurses at a hospital in Seattle. After being returned to prison, Harper was sent to the Special Offender Center (SOC). The initial diagnosis of Harper indicated that he was suffering from a manic-depressive disorder. He gave voluntary consent to treatment, including the administration of antipsychotic drugs, until November 1982 when he refused to continue taking his prescribed medication. His physician sought to continue his medication despite his objections, pursuant to SOC Policy 600.30. Policy 600.30 states that if a psychiatrist orders antipsychotic medication, an inmate may be involuntarily treated only if he (1) suffers from a "mental disorder" and (2) is "gravely disabled or poses a likelihood of serious harm" to himself or others. After a hearing in which the above conditions are met, a special committee consisting of a psychiatrist, a psychologist, and a Center official (none of whom may be currently involved in the inmate's treatment) can order involuntary medication if the psychiatrist is in the majority. The inmate has a right to notice of the hearing, the right to attend, present evidence, and cross-examine witnesses. He or she has a right to a disinterested lay advisor versed in psychological issues, the right to appeal to the Center's Superintendent, and the right to periodic review of any involuntary medication ordered. The inmate also has the right to judicial review of a committee decision in state court by means of a personal restraint petition, or extraordinary writ. The Court stated in *Harper* that given the prison environment, the due process clause permits the state to treat a prison inmate who has a serious mental illness with antipsychotic drugs against his will, if the inmate is dangerous to himself or others and the treatment is in the inmate's medical interests. As such,

Harper states that a prisoner with a serious mental illness may be treated with antipsychotic drugs against his will. There must be a hearing prior to such treatment, but the hearing does not have to be before a judge: a hearing before a special committee appointed by correctional officials is sufficient.

Harris v. Thigpen, 941 F.2d 1495 (11th Cir. 1991)

The Alabama prison system implemented a policy of mandatory human immune deficiency virus (HIV) testing of all inmates and for segregating those who were HIV positive. Alabama's program created many critics from both the inside, as well as the outside, of the prison system. In *Harris*, the district court agreed with the policy of mandatory testing of new admissions into the prison as an attempt to address the threat of the AIDS virus to the prison population. In this case, both the district and appeals courts held that segregating HIV-positive inmates does not constitute cruel and unusual punishment and does not require any procedural due process. HIV-positive inmates challenged the state's commitment to provide them with adequate treatment (zidovudine, or AZT) for AIDS. They argued that in the free community people with the AIDS virus were provided with adequate treatment and that they, because of their prison status, were not. The courts found that this was not a show of deliberate indifference to the medical needs of HIV- infected inmates since (AZT) was expensive. Further, a number of non-HIV infected inmates supported the prison policy of mandatory testing and segregating those with a positive HIV status, because of their fear of contracting the disease. The district court acknowledged the concerns of the non-HIV inmates but did not rule that they had a constitutional right to be tested and segregated. The court did not order the state to provide its program of segregating HIV-positive inmates as a constitutional entitlement for the inmates. HIV-positive inmates argued that being segregated because of their status would essentially exclude them from placement into programs, (such as vocational and educational jobs) and deny them access to the law library, work release, and other types of rehabilitation programs that could help them upon release. The inmates contended that such exclusion is a violation of the equal protection clause under the law. In *Harris*, the court said that prison officials use discretion to provide rehabilitation programs, but that inmates have no legal entitlement to such programs.

Wilson v. Seiter, 501 U.S. 294 (1991)

Wilson, an inmate at the Hocking Correctional Facility in Ohio, filed a

Section 1983 suit claiming that his Eighth Amendment right was violated by the treatment he received while confined. Wilson alleges that he was subjected to overcrowding, excessive noise, insufficient locker storage space, inadequate heating and cooling, improper ventilation, unclean and inadequate restrooms, unsanitary dining facilities and food preparation, and housing with mentally and physically ill inmates. In *Wilson*, the Court noted that the high standard noted in Whitley applied only to officials who were handling emergency situations. In the more general poor conditions cases, such as Wilson, the state of mind of prison officials would have to be shown to sustain a finding of cruel and unusual punishment. The Court said that it would have to be proven that officials acted with deliberate indifference to the basic needs of inmates. Moreover, it argued that each violation has to be examined individually to determine if officials acted with deliberate indifference. The Court reasoned that it was not proper to look at the "overall conditions" to decide whether there was cruel and unusual punishment. Therefore, prisoners contesting conditions of confinement in federal court must show that prison officials acted with deliberate indifference to a prisoner's needs and living.

Heflin v. Stewart County, 958 F.2d 709 (6th Cir. 1992)

In *Heflin*, the federal court of appeals upheld a jury award to the family of a jail inmate who hanged himself. Inmate Heflin was found hanging in his cell, but the Deputy Sheriff asked that his body remain hanging until a doctor or medical staff arrive to assist. When medical staff arrived 20 minutes after the discovery, Heflin was cut down but died soon afterwards. The appeals court argued that pretrial detainees have a constitutional right to the same protection afforded to convicted prisoners who have serious medical needs. In this case, the court of appeals and the trial court found that the Deputy Sheriff should have immediately cut down the inmate and administered CPR because he was still alive and the officer had been trained to conduct such procedures. The court stated that "the unlawfulness of doing nothing" to attempt to save Heflin's life would have been apparent to a reasonable official in the deputy's position. This ruling constituted a finding of negligence on the part of the deputy. Moreover, the case demonstrated a show of deliberate indifference toward the condition of the inmate.

Hudson v. McMillian, 60 L.W. 4151 (1992)

Inmate Hudson brought a Section 1983 lawsuit against a prison in Louisiana alleging that officers violated his Eighth Amendment right by subjecting him to cruel and unusual punishment when they beat him about the mouth, eyes, chest, and stomach while walking him from his cell to the prisoners' administrative lock-down area. The prisoner also alleges that the supervisor on duty witnessed the beating that he sustained and told the two officers "not to have too much fun." As a result of the beating, the prisoner suffered minor bruises and swelling of the face, mouth, and lips. Hudson also sustained loosened teeth and a cracked dental plate. The federal magistrate found excessive use of force by the officers and admonished the actions of the supervisor. The prisoner was awarded $800 in damages. The Fifth Circuit Court of Appeals reversed this judgement, holding that there was no violation of the Eighth Amendment prohibition against cruel and unusual punishment, because Hudson did not sustain "significant injuries," and the injuries that he sustained were minor and required no medical treatment. The Supreme Court held that the use of excessive physical force by prison officials against a prisoner may constitute cruel and unusual punishment, and is therefore unconstitutional, even if the inmate does not suffer serious injury. In *Hudson*, the Court stated that as long as excessive force is used "maliciously and sadistically" to cause harm, it violates the Eighth Amendment.

Blumhagen v. Sabes, 834 F. Supp. 1347 (D.Wyo. 1993)

In *Blumhagen*, an inmate in Wyoming filed a lawsuit alleging that prison officials had screened all inmates for tuberculosis (TB), but had failed to isolate the infectious TB cases. The inmate contended that a failure to isolate those with TB from those without it ran the risk of having those uninfected exposed to the disease. In this case, the federal district court held that the allegations showed only differences of opinion about how TB cases should be treated and the actions of Wyoming prison officials did not amount to a showing of deliberate indifference to the medical needs of the prisoners. However, the court did note that inmates might have a claim for malpractice under the Wyoming Tort law and suggested that the inmates look into that as a possible remedy.

Helling v. McKinney, 53 Cr.L. 2230 (1993)

McKinney, a Nevada state prisoner, filed a lawsuit under Section 1983 claiming that he was subjected to environmental tobacco smoke. The cause of his exposure was due to a cell mate who smoked five packs of cigarettes each day. The inmate alleged that he experienced health problems related to this exposure, which essentially constituted cruel and unusual punishment in violation of the Eighth Amendment. Both parties agreed to a jury trial before a magistrate. The magistrate held that the two issues to be considered were the inmate's constitutional right to be housed in a smoke-free environment and deliberate indifference on the part of prison officials to the inmate's serious medical needs. In *McKinney*, the Court held that a prisoner does not need to show that the conditions he challenged have caused current health problems, but rather that conditions posing serious threats to his future health are actionable. As a result, prison conditions that pose an alleged risk of harm to a prisoner's health, both at present and in the future, can be actionable under the Eighth Amendment's prohibition against cruel and unusual punishment. This case also gives prison administrators a great deal of authority to either ban smoking altogether or place serious control on the practice.

Reed v. Woodruff County, 7 F.3d 808 (8th Cir. 1993)

In this case, a prison trustee was found hanging in a shower stall where it was determined that he had died while engaging in auto-erotic asphyxiation--using hanging to bring about increased sexual gratification. In *Reed*, staff had discovered that the inmate was not in his cell. They had not found the inmate until after he had hung himself and died from sustained injuries. The surviving family members brought an action against the county jail, claiming that the inmate's death was the result of negligence and was therefore a violation of his constitutional rights. However, under Arkansas law, the county was immune from a negligence claim. In *Reed*, the family argued that the jailer who found the inmate should have made attempts to resuscitate the inmate and that the failure alone constituted a show of deliberate indifference to the plight of the inmate. The federal court rejected the claim, ruling instead that there was no obligation on the part of the jailer to revive the prisoner when the trained jailer had already determined that the inmate was dead. The court ruled that there was no evidence suggesting such an attempt at resuscitating the inmate would have succeeded, and therefore no constitutional violation was committed.

Farmer v. Brennan, 55 Cr.L. 2135 (1994)

Inmate Farmer, a transsexual, was transferred from a federal correctional institution to another prison where he was placed in the general population. Farmer has the appearance and demeanor of a woman, enhanced by silicone breast implants and female hormones, but had male sexual organs. Farmer was beaten and raped by another inmate after being transferred from one federal prison to another. He filed an action seeking damages and an injunction barring future confinement in the penitentiary. Farmer alleged that a prison official had acted with deliberate indifference toward his safety, thereby violating his Eighth Amendment right to be protected from cruel and unusual punishment. He contended that the prison official placed him in a violent environment and a setting with a history of violent sexual attacks. The Supreme Court disagreed with Farmer and held that for prison officials to be held liable, they must have "knowingly disregarded an excessive risk of harm." It is not enough that the official should have known that harm was inevitable, because the risk was so obvious that a reasonable person should have noticed it. In this case, the Court moved away from having inmates show that an official acted with deliberate indifference and created a new standard that will be very difficult for inmates to establish. This standard is very high. The word "knowing" in itself suggests that prison officials who are unaware of a risk that an inmate faces cannot be held liable for injuries the inmate sustains at the hands of other inmates.

Myers v. Lake County, 30 F.3d 847 (7th Cir. 1994)

In *Myers*, there was an attempted suicide by a 16-year-old juvenile detained in a county facility. As a result of the attempt, the detainee suffered permanent brain damage and was awarded $600,000 in a lawsuit alleging that the custodians had been negligent. In this case, an Indiana jury found that the detention facility was negligent in not taking adequate precautions against suicide attempts. The federal court of appeals upheld the judgement, concluding that state law required that facilities must use reasonable care to prevent suicides. Moreover, the court recognized that all suicides may not be prevented but reasonable steps must be taken to prevent them. The county argued that because of economic strain, suicide prevention strategies and staff were inadequate to ensure inmate safety. The court rejected this defense, contending that the county could not use a lack of funding as a defense when the claim against it is the failure to perform a required legal duty.

Gates v. Rowland, 39 F.3d 1439 (9th Cir. 1995)

In this case, the court of appeals held that California prison officials did not have to place HIV-positive inmates into work assignments in the area of food service. In *Gates*, the lower court enjoined the prison officials from denying those regular work assignments to HIV-positive inmates. The court of appeals reasoned that to allow HIV-infected inmates to work in the area of food preparation would create a perceived threat of exposure to and infection of the virus that causes AIDS. The court also ruled that maintaining positive attitudes among the inmates about the safety and sanitation of their food was important in the prison setting.

Jolly v. Coughlin, 894 F. Supp. 734 (S.D.N.Y. 1995)

Jolly, a Rastafarian inmate in New York, refused to take a TB screening test based on his religious beliefs. Pursuant to the corrections department's TB control program, any inmate who refused the test would be placed on "medical keeplock." Jolly was in keeplock status for more than three and a half years. He never displayed any symptoms of TB, and his three X-ray tests were negative. The court found that officials were substantially burdening Jolly's exercise of his religious beliefs and that there was not a compelling governmental interest that justified his prolonged status. In this case, prison officials did not convince the court that their means of dealing with Jolly was the least restrictive means of furthering the interest of preventing the spread of TB. Officials admitted that Jolly was not contagious. The court ordered Jolly's release from keeplock status and enjoined prison officials from placing him there.

Key Terms

conditions of death row
conditions of prison
deadly force
death penalty sentences
deprivation of basic needs
double ceiling
excessive force
hands-off approach
harsh sentences
medical treatment
reasonable force
SOC Policy 660.30

CASES CITED

Talley v. Stephens, 247 F. Supp. 683 E.D. Ark. (1965)
Jackson v. Bishop, 404 F.2d 371 8th Cir. 1068 (1968)
Holt v. Sarver, 300 F. Supp. 825 (E.D. Ark.) (1970)
Furman v. Georgia, 408 U.S. 238 (1972)
Logue v. United States, 412 U.S. 521 (1973)
Estelle v. Gamble, 429 U.S. 97 (1976)
Gregg v. Georgia, 428 U.S. 153 (1976)
Hutto v. Finney, 437 U.S. 678 (1978)
Ruiz v. Estelle, 503 F. Supp. 1265 S.D. Tex. (1980)
Rhodes v. Chapman, 452 U.S. 337 (1981)

City of Revere v. Massachusetts General Hospital, 463 U.S. 239 (1983)
Smith v. Wade, 33 Cr.L. 3021 (1983)
Whitley v. Albers, 106 S.Ct. 1078 (1986)
Doe v. Couglin, (D.C.N.Y. No. 88-CV-964) (1988)
Roe v. Fauver, 43 Cr.L. 2174 (1988)
West v. Atkins, 108 S.Ct. 2250 (1988)
Wood v. White, 689 F. Supp. 874 (W.D. Wis. 1988)
Washington v. Harper, 58 L.W. 4249 (1990)
Harris v. Thigpen, 941 F.2d 1495 (11th Cir. 1991)
Wilson v. Seiter, 501 U.S. 294 (1991)
Heflin v. Stewart County, 958 F.2d 709 (6th Cir.1992)
Hudson v. McMillian, 60 L. W. 4151 (1992)
Blumhagen v. Sabes, 834 F. Supp. 1347 (D.Wyo. 1993)
Helling v. McKinney, 53 Cr.L. 2230 (1993)
Reed v. Woodruff County, 7 F.3d 808 (8th Cir. 1993)
Farmer v. Brennan, 55 Cr.L. 2135 (1994)
Myers v. Lake County, 30 F.3d 847 (7th Cir. 1994)
Gates v. Rowland, 39 F.3d 1439 (9th Cir. 1995)
Jolly v. Coughlin, 894 F. Supp. 734 (S.D.N.Y. 1995)

REFERENCES

Adler, F., Mueller, G. O., and Laufer, W. S. (1994). Criminal Justice. New York: McGraw-Hill, Inc.

Cauchon, D. (1995). "AIDS in prison: Locked Up and Locked Out." USA Today, March 31, 1995:6A.

Centers for Disease Control and Prevention (1994). HIV/AIDS Surveillance Report. 9:1-5.

Cohen, F. (1992). Liability for Custodial Suicide: The Information Base Requirements. Jail Suicide Update. 4(2)1-11.

Collins, W. C. (1990). Correctional Law for the Correctional Officer. Washington, D.C.: St. Mary's Press.

Crawford, C. A. (1994). "Health Care Needs in Corrections: NIJ Responds." NIJ Journal (November):31.

Cripe, C. A. (1997). Legal Aspects of Corrections Management. Maryland: Aspen Publication.

del Carmen, R. V., (1991). Civil Liabilities in American Policing. Englewood Cliffs, N J: Prentice-Hall.

Dilulio, J. (1990). (ed). Courts, Corrections, and the Constitution: The Impact of Judicial Intervention on Prisons and Jails. New York: Oxford University Press.

Gilman, D. (1977). "Courts and Corrections." Corrections, March, p.47.

Kappeler, V.E. (1993). Critical Issues in Police Civil Liability. Prospect Heights, Illinois: Wave Land Press.

Kappeler, V.E., Vaughn, M. S., and del Carmen, R. V. (1991). Death in Detention: An Analysis of Police Liability for Negligent Failure to Prevent Suicide. Journal of Criminal Justice, 19(4) 381-394.

Sennott, C.M. (1994). "AIDS A Fatal Factor to Prison Assault: Rape Behind Bars." Boston Globe, May, 2.

CHAPTER 9

Inmates and the Fourteenth Amendment

FOCAL POINTS

- The Fourteenth Amendment
- Discussion of Due Process
- Discussion of Equal Protection
- Some Pertinent Cases
- Key Terms

Amendment XIV to the United States Constitution states:

> All persons born or naturalized in the United States, and subject to the jurisdiction thereof are citizens of the United States and of the State wherein they reside. No state shall make or enforce any law which shall abridge the privileges or immunities of citizens of the United States; nor shall any State deprive any person of life, liberty or property without due process of law; nor deny to any person within its jurisdiction the equal protection of the laws.

In the Constitution, due process is referred to twice. It is found in the Fifth and the Fourteenth Amendments. The Fifth Amendment's mention of due process is applicable to the federal government and the Fourteenth is applicable to the states. In matters of prison, state and local inmates are protected by the Fourteenth Amendment and federal inmates are protected by the Fifth Amendment. However, the majority of corrections cases that allege a due process claim are addressed by the Fourteenth Amendment. The Fourteenth Amendment was adopted after the Civil War to ensure that states would not arbitrarily try to take away the life, liberty, or property of its citizens.

The Fourteenth Amendment contains two clauses: due process and equal protection. First, due process of the law speaks to compliance with the fundamental rule for fair and orderly proceeding; for example, the opportunity to appear and be heard, the right to effective counsel and a fair and impartial jury. Due process is defined as those legal proceedings which observe the rules designed for the protection and enforcement of individual rights and liberties. The Constitution states that no State shall deprive a person of life, liberty, or property without due process of the law. Because of this, when it is established that one has an interest (a legal claim), the due process claim can be invoked. Again, the purpose of the Amendment is to ensure that states do not infringe on the rights of citizens. Second, equal protection of the law is designed to guarantee uniformity of treatment under the law of all persons in similar circumstances. It is usually applied to civil and political rights. This clause does not create new rights where none previously existed, except to those persons who may have been excluded from them.

The language of the Fourteenth Amendment addresses two items. First, it has to be established that a person has been deprived of life, liberty, or property, or has been adversely affected by the government's action. Second, once established, it must be determined what process is due the individual. Some scholars contend that the purpose of due process is to ensure that government has taken actions that are justified and has engaged in such action with procedural safeguards to ensure that the person is treated fairly. Courts have interpreted fairness to mean that the government must provide steps that will guarantee that the facts are as the government claims and that the action taken by the government is authorized by law. This is referred to as the process which is due to an individual if it is established first that there is an entitlement to a process.

Courts have also stated that the facts and circumstances involved in each case will determine the type of process that is due to the individual. For example, the courts have argued that the greater the loss that is involved, the more procedural protection an individual should be provided by the government. Within the prison settings, inmates often allege a liberty interest when they become involved in incidences. As such, courts have struggled to determine if the inmates' interests warrant due process protections, and if they do, what degree of protection should prisoners be provided. In prisons, some actions carry a high degree of procedural protection, but there are others that carry a low or no degree of protection, even when inmates allege that they were subjected to a deprivation by the government (Cripe, 1997).

When inmates are involved in rule infractions or crimes committed within the context of confinement, and actions are taken against them, they usually challenge such allegations. Inmates claim that they have an interest in proving their innocence. For example, when prisoners face disciplinary actions, they argue that they have a liberty interest, and as such, they should be afforded due process. They base such claims on the fact that a finding of guilt could adversely affect them. They argue that (1) an action against them could prolong their sentence, (2) property could be taken from them or they could be forced to pay off items that they have damaged, (3) the conditions of their confinement could change, i.e. placement in administrative or punitive segregation, isolation, or even transfer, and (4) privileges (visitation and recreation) that they enjoy could be revoked or discontinued.

According to Cripe (1997), there are several types of actions that prisoners could potentially face. First, a report of serious misconduct to a parole board could deny an inmate's release. Second, accumulated "good time" could be taken away from an inmate, requiring him or her to serve out the remainder of an original sentence. Third, an inmate could be placed in disciplinary segregation. Fourth, his or her property and privileges could be withheld. Fifth, an assignment to a preferred job or housing could be changed. Sixth, an inmate could be transferred to another prison with the same or greater security level. Given this situation, prisoners argue they have a legitimate entitlement to due process because a guilty finding can adversely affect their status.

In the past, inmates were subjected to many harsh realities and practices at the hands of prison administrators. Correctional administrators had long been free to dispense administrative punishments for disciplinary infractions. Prisoners would often have privileges revoked, be denied right of access to counsel, sit in solitary or administrative segregation, or lose accrued "good time" because of a single unreviewed report by a correctional guard. This occurred because the courts used to defer to the administrator's discretion -- the final word on reasonable prison practices (Cole, 1989). Critics charged that the unreviewed discretion of prison officials was the greatest evil inmates faced, not inmate violence, homosexuality, or the physical brutality of correctional guards. This practice is no longer the case.

Currently, inmates must be afforded due process and equal protection under the law to ensure that they are not subjected to any arbitrary abuse. They now have due process and equal protection guarantees. In the past, violation of a rule or suspicion of violation could result in a prisoner being physically beaten, placed in solitary confinement, or deprived of accumulated "good time" without notification of charges pending against him or her. The inmate was not allowed to challenge allegations by producing evidence or witnesses to support his or her innocence. Those days are long gone. Though inmates do not enjoy the same due process and equal protection as people in the free community, the courts have made some efforts to protect the interests of those who are confined. Under the Fourteenth Amendment, no one should be deprived of life, liberty, or property without due process of law. Therefore, inmates often assert when their liberty is in jeopardy (disciplinary or administrative segregation), that they should be made aware of charges through written notification and afforded the opportunity to prove their innocence. At the same time, if property is taken away or if they face the prospect of having good time taken away, inmates are entitled to due process.

The U.S. participates in international transfers. International transfer programs began in 1977 between the U.S. and Canada and continued with other countries. The purpose of an international transfer is to place a visiting prisoner closer to his home country so that he can be under the supervision of the laws and in the custody of his own country. As a result, the U.S. has created treaties with several countries (Canada, Mexico, Bolivia, France, Marshall Islands, Palau, Peoria, Thailand, Turkey, and others) to return their citizens and have U.S. citizens transferred from these respective countries. These bilateral treaties have their basis in **Title 18 of the U.S. Code, Section 4100**. Transfers are conducted through the Department of Justice. Before a country can transfer a prisoner, there are several conditions that must be met. Cripe (1997) contends that the conditions of international transfer are (1) only prisoners whose criminal offenses would be considered violations in their home country, (2) the transfer would have to be agreed to by all parties involved (visiting, home country, and the prisoner), (3) the conviction and sentence must be recognized by the home country, (4) all appeals of conviction and sentence must be exhausted before transfer, and (5) the prisoner must still have a reasonable amount of time to serve before transfer. Despite these conditions that must be met before they can be released and transferred to their home country, some prisoners, upon arrival to their native soil, try to challenge the legality of their sentence and confinement status, contending that they are entitled to due process.

Some Pertinent Cases

Baxter v. Palmigiano
Cleavinger v. Saxner
Daniel v. Williams
Davidson v. Cannon
Hewitt v. Helms
Howe v. Smith
Hudson v. Palmer
Lee v. Washington
Marquez Ramon v. Reno

Meachum v. Fano
Montanye v. Haymes
Muhammad v. Carlson
Olim v. Wakinekona
Parratt v. Taylor
Ponte v. Real
Rosada v. Civiletti
Sandin v. Conner
United States v. Gouveia
Superintendent v. Hill
United States v. Bailey
Vitek v. Jones
Wolff v. McDonnell

Lee v. Washington, 390 U.S. 333 (1968)

Inmates in the Alabama Department of Corrections (ADC) filed an action for declaratory and injunctive relief over racial segregation in the Alabama prison system, including county and local jails. The inmates claimed that racial segregation is a violation of the Fourteenth Amendment's equal protection clause. The Commissioner of the ADC argued that racial segregation was necessary to maintain security and order. The Supreme Court held that racial segregation in prison was a constitutional violation under the equal protection clause of the Fourteenth Amendment. However, the Court held that prison administrators have the right, in particular circumstances, to take race into account if it means that it will allow them to better maintain security, discipline, and good order of jails and prisons. This is provided that prison administrators are acting in good faith.

Wolff v. McDonnell, 418 U.S. 539 (1974)

Inmates at a Nebraska prison filed a complaint for damages and an injunction under Section 1983 in which they alleged that the Nebraska prison disciplinary proceedings violated their constitutional right to due process. Under Nebraska's disciplinary procedure, forfeiture or withholding of good time credits or confinement in a disciplinary cell is the penalty imposed for serious misconduct. To establish misconduct (1) a preliminary conference is held with the chief corrections supervisor and the charging party, in which the prisoner is orally informed of the charge and the merits are preliminarily discussed, (2) a conduct report is prepared and a hearing held before the prison's disciplinary body, which is composed of three prison officials, and (3) the inmate may ask questions of the charging party. The issue in *Wolff* was, is due process required in prison disciplinary proceedings? The Supreme Court said that inmates are entitled to due process in prison disciplinary proceedings that can result in the loss of good time credits or in punitive segregation. Due process in a prison disciplinary proceeding requires the following:

(1) Advance written notice of the charges against the inmate must be given to him at least 24 hours before his appearance before the prison disciplinary board.

(2) There must be a written statement by the fact finder as to the evidence relied upon and reasons for the disciplinary action.

(3) The inmate should be allowed to call witnesses and present documentary evidence in his defense, providing there is no undue hazard to institutional safety or correctional goals.

(4) There may be counsel substitute (either a fellow inmate, if permitted, or staff), where the inmate is illiterate or where the complexity of the issues make it unlikely that the inmate will be able to collect and present the evidence for an adequate comprehension of the case.

(5) The prison disciplinary board must be impartial.

The following is not constitutionally required:

(1) The inmate is not entitled to confrontation and cross examination. The permitting of these activities is left to the discretion of the disciplinary board.

(2) The inmate has no constitutional right to retained or appointed counsel. The decision is not retroactive. There is no right to expungement or prior disciplinary proceeding. The decision is applicable only to those cases involving serious misconduct. A less formal standard is applicable to other proceedings.

Baxter v. Palmigiano, 425 U.S. 308 (1976)

In this case, the Court considered two cases (*Enomoto v. Clutchette* and *Baxter v. Palmigiano*) at the same time concerning disciplinary issues. Both of these cases had made it to the court of appeals. Enomoto is considered as a companion case to *Baxter*. The Court disagreed with the decisions of the courts of appeals and upheld its decision in *Wolff v. McDonnell* that inmates do not have the right to either retained or appointed counsel in disciplinary hearings that are not part of a criminal prosecution, nor to confront or cross examine witnesses. The Court also held that an inmate's decision to assert the Fifth Amendment and remain silent at a disciplinary proceeding can be given adverse evidentiary significance.

Meachum v. Fano, 427 U.S. 215 (1976)

The Massachusetts Correctional Institution at Norfolk (a medium security prison) experienced nine serious fires during two-and-one half months. During this time, the Classification Board conducted a hearing and decided that inmate Royce be placed in administrative segregation for 30 days, because of his involvement in setting the fires. Inmates Fano, Dussault, and McPhearson were to be transferred to Walpole (a maximum security prison) where living conditions were more unfavorable than those at Norfolk. Inmates DeBrosky and Hathaway were to be transferred to Bridgewater (which has both medium and maximum security facilities). The meeting with the Classification Board included Acting Duty Commissioner of Classification and Treatment and the Commissioner of Corrections. They recommended transferring the inmates to other facilities. In this case, inmates brought a Section 1983 claim alleging that by being transferred to an institution where living conditions were less favorable, they were deprived of their liberty interests under due process found in the Fourteenth Amendment. The Court disagreed and argued that when inmates are transferred from a medium to a maximum security facility, they are not entitled to a fact-finding hearing. The Court also stated that the due process clause is satisfied when defendants receive a valid conviction in a court of law. After sentence is imposed, the prisoners are confined by the state and must comport to its rules and regulations. The due process clause does not protect a prisoner from being transferred to another prison in the same state. In this case, the Court also maintained that as long as transferring prisoners is discretionary under state law, there is no need to give inmates a hearing or other due process rights. Prison officials had discretionary power to transfer any inmate.

Montanye v. Haymes, 427 U.S. 236 (1976)

In this case, Haymes, an inmate at the Attica Correctional Facility (a maximum security prison) in New York was dismissed as a clerk in the law library. After his dismissal, he was observed circulating a petition with the signatures of 82 inmates. The petition protested inmates' deprivation of legal assistance as a result of Haymes' dismissal as clerk. The petition was seized by prison guards. The following day, Haymes was informed that he had been transferred to another prison facility, Clinton Correctional Facility (a maximum security facility). Despite the transfer, no disciplinary actions were taken against Haymes. Haymes filed a petition in the United States District Court seeking relief against Montanye (the Superintendent of Attica). Haymes claimed that the seizure and retention of his petition violated Administrative Bulletin No. 20 and infringed on his ability to address the court for a redress of grievance. The question in this case was, does the due process clause of the Fourteenth Amendment require that a hearing be given if a state prisoner is transferred to another institution in the state, even if the transfer is not disciplinary or punitive? In keeping with its decision given in *Meachum*, the Court argued that if state law does not prohibit such transfers, prison officials can transfer prisoners from one prison to another without giving them due process. Moreover, in this case, the Court stated that persons sentenced to prisons are not sentenced to particular institutions, but are committed to the custody by the Commissioner of Corrections. The Commissioner is empowered by statue to transfer inmates from one facility to another.

Rosada v. Civiletti, 621 F.2d 1179 (2d Cir. 1980)

In this case, Rosada and three other U.S. citizens had been arrested and imprisoned in Mexico on charges of narcotics violations. After their arrest, they contended that they were subjected to being stripped, bound, beaten, and tortured with electricity. They were provided no access to a lawyer or allowed to communicate with family members. They refused to sign confessions that were prepared for them by prison authorities and were subsequently transferred into a regular prison where, they contend, they were told that they would have to pay $2,000 for their cell and other amenities. After a month, they were taken to court and asked to confirm the statements that prosecuting officials had prepared for them. They refused and were returned to prison. They were later told that despite their efforts to deny the charges, the judge had found them guilty of drug offenses and each was sentenced to nine years of imprisonment. Rosada and others, after being returned to the U.S., challenged the validity of their confinement and transfer on the basis that their original conviction was invalid because they had been afforded no access to see the judge, to have an attorney, and to bring witnesses on their behalf. The Court of Appeals disagreed and upheld the constitutionality of the transfer procedure. In this case, the court argued that the Constitution and Bill of Rights were designed to protect the interest and rights of offenders in America, not those in Mexico, and as such they do not protect U.S. citizens against the actions of other countries.

United States v. Bailey, 40.78-990 (1980)

In *Bailey*, four inmates escaped from a jail in the District of Columbia allegedly to avoid the coercive and intolerable conditions of confinement there, such as frequent fires, inadequate medical care, beatings, and death threats from guards. After this evidence was introduced at trial on escape charges, the defendants requested that the district court instruct the jury on the defense of duress so that they could consider whether the deplorable conditions justified or mitigated the crime. In *Bailey*, the Supreme Court ruled that the defendants were not entitled to claim duress and be exonerated on those grounds, because after escaping they had not made any efforts to surrender to authorities. The Court concluded that their failure to turn themselves in or to satisfactorily explain their continued flight from custody discredited any affirmative defense to escape. *Bailey* signifies that if escapees surrender immediately or make a genuine effort to do so, juries may receive instruction on the duress defense and indeed decide that such inmates had a "right" to escape under the circumstances.

Vitek v. Jones, 445 U.S. 480 (1980)

Jones, a Nebraska prison inmate, was convicted of robbery and was transferred to the penitentiary hospital seven months after he was sentenced to prison. After two days in the hospital he was placed in solitary confinement. While there, he set his mattress on fire, severely burning himself. The burn unit of a private hospital treated him and he was then transferred to the security unit of the Lincoln Regional Center, a state mental hospital that was run by the Department of Public Institutions. Jones was transferred to the mental hospital under a Nebraska statute, which states that when a designated physician or psychologist finds that a prisoner "suffers from a mental disease or defect" and "cannot be given proper treatment in that facility," the Director of Corrections may transfer him for examination, study, and treatment to another institution, whether or not it is within the Department of Correctional Services. Jones was found to be suffering from a mental illness or defect for which he could not receive proper treatment in the penal institution. As a result, the transfer was ordered. Jones then intervened in this case, which was brought by other prisoners against the appropriate state officials, including Vitek, the Director of Corrections. The case challenged the Nebraska statute, which permitted transfer of prisoners from the complex to a mental hospital without procedural due process, as a violation of the Fourteenth Amendment. In *Vitek*, the Court stated that the involuntary transfer of a prisoner to a mental hospital implicates a liberty interest that is protected by the due process clause of the Fourteenth Amendment. Although a conviction and sentence extinguish an individual's right to freedom for the term of his sentence, they do not authorize the state to classify him as mentally ill and subject him to involuntary psychiatric treatment without affording him additional due process protections. These protections should include:

1. A written notice to the prisoner that such a transfer is being considered;

2. A full hearing held after a reasonable period has passed to allow the prisoner to prepare for it;

3. An opportunity for the prisoner to present witnesses at his hearing, and when feasible, the opportunity to cross-examine witnesses called by the state;

4. An independent decision-maker to preside over the hearing;

5. A written statement to the prisoner citing the evidence and reasons for the transfer; and

6. Advisement of all the prisoner's procedural rights.

The Court found that the transfer of a prisoner from a prison to a mental hospital must be accompanied by appropriate procedural protections. The transfer implicates a liberty interest that is protected by the due process clause, because of the stigmatizing consequences of a transfer to a mental hospital. It typically involves involuntary psychiatric treatment.

Howe v. Smith, 452 U.S. 473 (1981)

The Vermont Commissioner of Corrections announced that he would closed the State Prison at Windsor (the only maximum security prison in the state). This would leave only community correctional centers and the Diagnostic Treatment Facility at St. Albans as state correctional facilities for adult inmates inside the state. The community correctional centers were for minimum security inmates. Inmate Howe was serving a sentence of life for murder. The Department of Corrections Classification Committee decided that he should be kept in a maximum security prison.

Therefore, he would have to be transferred to a federal prison. The Federal Bureau of Prisons had agreed to take up to 40 Vermont prisoners. This was done pursuant to 18 U.S.C. 5003(a) which allowed the Director of the Bureau of Prisons to take state prisoners upon certification that there were federal facilities that could accommodate them. Howe was given a hearing in Vermont with advance notice of the proposal and the reason for the recommendation. The hearing officer recommended that Howe be transferred to a federal institution, because Howe was dangerous and could not be placed into a community-based program. Moreover, the hearing officer also argued that Howe was an escape risk and had escaped from a maximum security facility in the past. The hearing officer argued that Howe needed long-term maximum security supervision. The Court upheld the transfer, stating that the federal statute that authorizes the Bureau of Prisons to take state prisoners makes the transfer valid and there is no basis for a challenge.

Parratt v. Taylor, 451 U.S. 527 (1981)

Inmate Taylor was confined at the Nebraska Penal and Correctional Complex. He ordered some hobby materials that cost him $23.50. Somehow, the materials got lost and he never received them. Taylor brought a lawsuit under Section 1983 contending that his property had been taken from him without due process of law. In this case, the Court addressed two questions. First, was the loss caused by someone acting under the color of law? Second, did the state official's conduct deprive Taylor of a right given to him under the Constitution? The Court found that Taylor had been deprived of his property under color of law. Thus, the first question was settled. However, the Court was not satisfied with the second question. The Court argued that the due process clause is not satisfied because Nebraska had a state tort claim procedure that would have served as a remedy for *Taylor*. Taylor chose not to avail himself of the remedy. The Court argued that the tort procedures would have defrayed the cost of the lost property and thus satisfied the requirement of due process. However, if Nebraska had not had this remedy in place, a due process claim could have been made.

Hewitt v. Helms, 459 U.S. 460 (1983)

In this case, Helms was removed from the general population and placed in administrative segregation at the Huntingdon, Pennsylvania State Correctional Institution. This occurred because of a major disruption at the institution that involved several assaults on prison officers and destruction of property. Helms was removed from his cell after order was restored and was placed in segregation for questioning during the investigation of the riot. He was afforded a minimal hearing five days after being placed in segregation. Helms contends that his removal warranted a due process protection. In this case, the Court stated that a transfer to a less favorable location for nonpunitive reasons is well within the terms of punishment ordinarily contemplated by a prison sentence. Moreover, the Court concluded that placement in a restrictive segregated place did not create a liberty interest. Therefore, Helms did not have a due process claim found within the meaning of the Constitution.

Olim v. Wakinekona, 416 U.S. 238 (1983)

Inmate Wakinekona was serving a life sentence in the Hawaii State Prison. Because he was a serious troublemaker, a Program Committee recommended his transfer to a prison on the mainland. He was later transferred to Folsom State Prison in California. Wakinekona filed a Section 1983 lawsuit against state officials on the grounds that he had been denied due process because he was not given a hearing before being transferred. The question in this case was, does due process protect an inmate against interstate transfer? The Court argued that Hawaii had policies in place that allowed the transfer of inmates into state and federal prisons outside of the state. The policies also permitted the transfer of inmates to other institutions in cases of prison overcrowding or if the inmate was a troublemaker. The Court, relying on its decisions in *Meachum* and *Montayne*, argued that an inmate has a justifiable expectation that he will be incarcerated in any particular state just as he should not have a justifiable expectation that he will be placed into a particular prison within a state.

Hudson v. Palmer, 468 U.S. 517 (1984)

In this case, inmate Palmer claimed that officers who searched his cell destroyed some of his personal property just to harass him. The Supreme Court extended its holding in *Parratt*, saying that even though there was a claim of intentional destruction of Palmer's property, the requirements of due process had been met in this case, because the state of Virginia gave Palmer a remedy. The Court said that Palmer could have filed a claim for compensation for his lost or damaged property. Because of this remedy, it precluded Palmer from bringing a constitutional deprivation suit under Section 1983. The Court said in this case that even intentional damage of property is not the basis for a constitutional claim when the damage of property is not the basis for a constitutional claim when the state has a remedy that inmates can use to be compensated for damaged property.

United States v. Gouveia, 467 U.S. 180 (1984)

In this case, Gouveia, a federal inmate, was placed in administrative segregation for 19 months while authorities investigated the murder of an inmate. He remained in segregation until he was indicted and arraigned in a federal court. Gouveia argued that during the time of his detainment, he was not provided counsel, a violation of his Sixth Amendment rights. However, the trial court denied that claim and he was convicted of murder. The Ninth Circuit Court of Appeals reversed his conviction, contending that Gouveia should have been given counsel after being placed in detention after 90 days or else be released back into the general population. The Supreme Court reversed the lower court ruling and said that Gouveia was not entitled to an appointed counsel while in administrative segregation. The Court said that the right to counsel attaches only at or after the initiation of adverse judicial proceedings against the defendant.

Cleavinger v. Saxner, 106 S.Ct. 496 (1985)

David Saxner and Alfred Cain, Jr., inmates at the Federal Correctional Institute in Terre Haute, Indiana, were found guilty by a prison disciplinary committee of encouraging other inmates to engage in a work stoppage and of other charges. They were ordered to be placed in administrative detention and to forfeit some of their accumulated "good-time." After appealing the matter to the Regional Director of the Bureau of Prisons, the inmates were ordered released from administrative detention and the inquiry expunged from their records. They were later granted parole and were subsequently released. They filed suit in federal court alleging a violation of their due process rights and were awarded damages. The members of the prison disciplinary committee objected and argued that like any other judicial body, they could not be sued because they enjoyed absolute immunity. In this case, the Court ruled that members of a prison disciplinary board do not enjoy absolute immunity, and therefore may be held liable for what they do. They enjoy only qualified immunity, meaning that they are immune from liability only if they acted in good faith. The Court argued that though prison disciplinary boards do perform "an adjudicatory function in that they hear testimony and receive documentary evidence, and in that they render a decision," they nonetheless are not in the same category as judges and therefore should not be given absolute immunity.

Ponte v. Real, 37 Cr.L. 3051 (1985)

If disciplinary officials refuse to call witnesses for an inmate at a disciplinary hearing and such refusal is challenged, they must at some point explain their refusal. But the reasons need not be written or made part of the administrative record of the hearing or they may decide to explain later in court if the prisoner alleges that the denial of witnesses deprived him or her of a "liberty" interest.

Superintendent v. Hill, 472 U.S. 445 (1985)

Inmate Hill was found guilty of assault based on testimony given by a prison guard. The guard stated that he heard some commotion, went over to investigate, and found an assaulted inmate. He saw Hill and two other inmates running away. No other inmates were in the area. He charged the three inmates with the assault. The disciplinary board also considered the guard's written report. They charged and found the inmates guilty of the assault. Hill lost 100 days of good time and was placed in isolation for 15 days. He filed suit in state court, which found insufficient evidence to support the finding of guilt. The Massachusetts Supreme Court affirmed that ruling. The U.S. Supreme Court reversed the decision of the Massachusetts court. In this case, the Court addressed what degree of evidence was required to support a finding of guilt in a prison disciplinary hearing. The Court argued that though the evidence in this case was minimal, it was sufficient to satisfy the low levels of protection required in prison hearings.

Daniel v. Williams, 474 U.S. 327 (1986)

Inmate Daniel brought a Section 1983 claim seeking damages for injuries to his back and ankle that he sustained when he fell on a stairway at the city jail in Richmond, Virginia. He alleged that a jail officer had acted negligently when he left a pillow on the stairs, which caused his fall. Daniel contended that this action deprived him of a liberty interest to be free from bodily injury. In this case, the Court held that a state official's negligent act that causes unintended loss of life, liberty, or property does not implicate the due process clause. The Court also held that the due process clause was intended to secure individuals from others, whether negligence is enough to state a constitutional claim.

Davidson v. Cannon, 474 U.S. 344 (1986)

Davidson was an inmate in New Jersey State Prison. He sent a note to the Assistant Superintendent saying that he had been threatened by another inmate. The Assistant Superintendent sent it to a corrections sergeant who failed to read the note right away and then left the prison. After being assaulted by the inmate, Davidson brought a Section 1983 suit alleging that his constitutional rights had been violated under the Eighth and Fourteenth Amendments. The District Court ruled that the prison officials had failed to take reasonable steps to protect Davidson and he was injured as a result of their failure. Using the standard established in *Parratt*, the district court found that Davidson was deprived of his liberty interest in his personal security and that New Jersey did not have a law or procedure that could compensate him for his injury. The trial court stated that he was deprived of a liberty interest and awarded damages of $2,000 against prison officials. The Court of Appeals reversed the lower court's judgment. The Supreme Court agreed to review the case. The Court said that where a government official is merely negligent in causing an injury, no procedure for compensation is constitutionally required. The Court also argued that the Constitution does not require prison officials to use due care in every situations, and it does not guarantee that officials will not make mistakes or be intentionally negligent. *Daniel v. Williams* and *Davidson v. Cannon* were decided on the same day.

Muhammad v. Carlson, 43 Cr.L. 2131 (1988)

Inmate Muhammad was transferred to a medical center, because he had lost his limb coordination. Blood examination indicated that he had AIDS. After being diagnosed, he was transferred to the general prison population and placed into isolation for seven months. Muhammad appealed his confinement, contending that it violated his right to due process in violation of the Fourteenth Amendment. In *Muhammad*, the appeals court upheld the constitutionality of his isolation, stating that the transfer was not intended to punish him and that such a transfer was conducted in a manner consistent with constitutional safeguards and with prison policy.

Marquez Ramon v. Reno, 69 F. 3d 477 (10th Cir. 1995)

Ramon, a Mexican national serving a sentence in a federal prison, sought a **writ of mandamus** asking that the court order the U.S. Attorney General to transfer him to Mexico. The court noted that under the Treaty on the Exercise of Penal Sentences between the U.S. and Mexico, a request for transfer by an inmate is to be conducted by the transferring country to the receiving country, but only if the transferring country views it as appropriate. The Treaty in the U.S. gives transferring authority to the Attorney General to use as a matter of discretion. In this case, the Attorney General denied Ramon's transfer request, because of his criminal actions and the ties that he had with the U.S. In this case, the district court and the court of appeal agreed that Ramon had no entitlement to mandamus relief because the Treaty gave the Attorney General total discretion to make such transfers.

Sandin v. Conner, 115 S.Ct. 2293 (1995)

In this case, Hawaii inmate Conner was charged with serious misconduct and was found guilty of the charges before an adjustment committee. Conner was sentenced to 30 days in disciplinary segregation. He was not allowed to call witnesses to testify at his hearing before the committee. Conner complained that being sentenced to disciplinary segregation would adversely affect the parole board decision to grant his release. The Ninth Circuit Court of Appeals argued that Conner had a liberty interest in remaining free from disciplinary segregation and that he had not received the due process required by *Wolff* when he was prohibited from presenting witnesses on his behalf. The Supreme Court reversed the judgment of the appeals court. The Court stated that neither the Hawaii prison regulation in question nor the due process clause afforded Conner a protected liberty interest that would entitle him to the procedural protections set forth in *Wolff.* Moreover, the Court noticed that in Hawaii the parole board is not required to deny parole for a misconduct record an inmate may get in prison. The parole board has procedural protections at its hearing that allow the inmate to explain his misconduct record. Because of this mechanism, the inmate is not denied due process, and no additional protection is needed at the prisoner's disciplinary hearing.

Key Terms

due process of law
equal protection of law

good time
international transfers

CASES CITED

Lee v. Washington, 390 U.S. 333 (1968)
Wolff v. McDonnell, 418 U.S. 539 (1974)
Baxter v. Palmigiano, 425 U.S. 308 (1976)
Meachum v. Fano, 427 U.S. 215 (1976)
Montanye v. Haymes, 427 U.S. 236 (1976)
Rosada v. Civiletti, 621 F.2d 1179 (2d Cir. 1980)
United States v. Bailey, 40.78-990 (1980)
Vitek v. Jones, 445 U. S. 480 (1980)
Howe v. Smith, 452 U.S. 473 (1981)
Parratt v. Taylor, 451 U.S. 527 (1981)
Hewitt v. Helms, 459 U.S. 460 (1983)
Olim v. Wakinekona, 416 U.S. 238 (1983)
Hudson v. Palmer, 468 U.S. 517 (1984)
United States v. Gouveia, 467 U.S. 180 (1984)
Cleavinger v. Saxner, 106 S.Ct. 496 (1985)
Ponte v. Real, 37 Cr.L. 3051 (1985)
Superintendent v. Hill, 472 U.S. 445 (1985)
Daniel v. Williams, 474 U.S. 327 (1986)
Davidson v. Cannon, 474 U.S. 344 (1986)
Muhammad v. Carlson, 43 Cr.L. 2131 (1988)
Marquez Ramon v. Reno, 69 F. 3d 477 (10th Cir. 1995)
Sandin v. Conner, 115 S.Ct. 2293 (1995)

REFERENCES

Cole, G. F. (1989). The American System of Criminal Justice. Pacific Grove, CA: Brooks/Cole Publishers.

Cripe, C. A. (1997). Legal Aspects of Corrections Management. Maryland: Aspen Publication.

Title 18 of the U.S. Code, Section 4100.

CHAPTER 10

Reverting to a Hands-off Approach

FOCAL POINTS

- Reverting to a Hands-off Approach
- Prison Litigation Reform Act of 1995
- A Decline in the Issuance of Habeas Corpus
- *Turner v. Safley* Revisited
- Key Terms

Some scholars argue that the wave of prison litigation that was widespread in the 1970s and 1980s was a reaction, in part, to the appellate courts' understanding of the cultural contexts found within society in general, and in places of confinement in particular. As mentioned earlier, the struggle for social justice in America by disenfranchised groups spilled over from the free community into places of confinement. Anderson and Newman (1993) contend that since places of confinement were disproportionately populated by cultural and ethnic minorities during the 1960s, mounting concerns grew in places of confinement, as well as the free community, over protecting the civil rights and constitutional safeguards of those who were imprisoned. These same scholars contend that in the year 2000, the need no longer exists for the federal courts to have such an active participation in ensuring the constitutional protections and safeguards of inmates. For example, del Carmen, Ritter, and Witt (1998) argue that prior to 1969, the Supreme Court had decided only one case in the area of prisoners' rights. However, from 1969 through 1995, the Court decided over forty-five cases involving prisoners' rights. After

1995, the Court has not decided any cases in the area of prisoner rights. While this fact does not suggest that there is social, political, or economic parity in society, it does mean that the Court and Congress may feel that the existing state of prisoners' rights, unlike the past, reflects a more compassionate and humane society. As a result, some believe that a move towards a hands-off approach to many of the claims now made by inmates has occurred. One cannot say that inmate claims will never be heard by the courts. However, the cases that are heard will be fewer in number and will go through a scanning process before they reach the Court.

Recent actions by the U.S. Supreme Court, as well as Congress signal a return to the hands-off doctrine. For example, the Rehnquist Court has made it a standing practice to deny certiorari, thus making it more difficult for inmates to have their claims heard by the Court. Recently, the Court has made it more difficult to challenge prison conditions in federal court. Similarly, Congress in 1996 limited federal court supervision of state prisons. These decisions clearly give prison administrators control over the operations and policies of their institutions. Moreover, state and federal legislation and the Court's efforts appear to adversely impact inmate litigation. The move from judicial activism to judicial inertia is seen even more clearly through, the Prison Litigation Reform Act of 1995, the decline of issuing the Writ of Habeas Corpus, and the case of *Turner v. Safley*.

PRISON LITIGATION REFORM ACT of 1995

As mentioned in Chapter Four of this book, Section 1983 litigations have been the favored remedy that prisoners use to have their complaints addressed. This remedy is believed to be favored among inmates because it offers injunctions, declaratory relief, pays damages if inmates prevail in court, and provides for attorney fees. Some critics of this type of litigation contend that since the federal courts have been receptive towards hearing inmate claims, the overwhelming number of inmate cases involve the use of Section 1983 challenges. Because of the increasing number (many of which, critics feel, are frivolous), the Court and federal government have come to view Section 1983 claims as an abuse of the system and an affront to legal access to the courts. As such, the federal government has addressed this problem through the passage of the Prison Litigation Reform Act of 1995. The Act was signed into law in 1996. According to the Act:

> No action shall be brought with respect to prison conditions under Section 1983 or any other federal law, by a prisoner confined in any jail, prison, or other correctional facility until such

administrative remedies as are available are exhausted.

The Act basically states that a court can suspend a Section 1983 claim if an inmate fails to exhaust all available grievance systems that are in place. The main purpose of the Act is to reduce the number of state prisoners' rights cases brought by the courts. More specifically, the Act is intended to reduce all trivial and frivolous claims that inmates use to flood the courts. Many scholars view the Prison Litigation Reform Act of 1995 as having an adverse affect on inmates, because it represents an erosion to Section 1983 litigation that inmates have enjoyed for several decades. Some see the new provisions of Section 1983 as a means by which the federal courts are closing the door on some inmates and making access to the courts more limited. In essence, the federal government has taken the prisoners' preferred remedy of choice away from them and placed limitations on their ability to bring their complaints about conditions of confinement to federal court. By requiring prisoners to use alternative methods for having their claims resolved before filing in the federal courts, it almost guarantees that many inmate claims will go unheard by the court, since they will be eliminated or resolved within the confines of correctional settings. If inmates fail to follow what is essentially a chain of command, their claims can be suspended without judicial review by federal courts. Notwithstanding, where state remedies are available to an inmate to file a grievance or claim, this could eliminate the case load of the federal courts. For example, inmates have been known to file Section 1983 claims to remedy situations where correctional officers destroy their property. The federal courts are saying that prisoners can have these types of issues more effectively addressed under state tort law.

THE DECLINE of ISSUING the WRIT of HABEAS CORPUS

Some critics argue that the Rehnquist Court is closing the federal doors on granting inmates relief through issuing the Writ of Habeas Corpus For many inmates who believe that they are illegally detained or wrongly sentenced, the Writ of Habeas Corpus symbolizes the only hope they may have for freedom or life. The writ is a constitutionally mandated vehicle that the falsely accused can use for release, but it is also commonly used by death row prisoners. The writ guarantees prisoners the opportunity to petition the federal courts to ensure that state courts do not make an error in deciding their conviction. Surprisingly to some, the Supreme Court, Congress, and the President are now placing restrictions on its use. This comes as disappointing news to inmates in jail and to prisoners incarcerated in total institutions. It represents a set back in prisoners' ability to seek release from confinement through the writ of habeas corpus. In deciding to place restrictions on its usage, there is a balancing test that occurs. For example, the courts must balance the rights of the offender (for freedom or to delay the inevitable if he sits on death row) against the needs of society to bring closure or finality to a case. Friedman (1995) argues that continuing habeas corpus is taxing to society. It causes a burden on judicial resources, family members' grief, prevents the idea of fairness, and further erodes the deterrent effect of punishment.

Cheurprakobkit and Theis (1999) argue that in recent years the Court has made it more difficult for prisoners to file habeas corpus petitions by following the cause and prejudice standard that is highlighted in *Wainwright v. Sykes*. However, they contend that *Teague v. Lane* has had the greatest impact in eroding relief under habeas corpus. Prior to *Teague*, habeas corpus was actively used by the courts in creating new rules of criminal procedure. Since its ruling, habeas corpus is used by the Supreme Court to deny petitions and chasten state courts for deviating from the Constitution. Moreover, Cheurprakobkit and Theis contend that these similar sentiments of the use of habeas corpus are also reflected by Congress and the President. Congress voted for ending funding for the death penalty centers program (providing legal representation for death penalty inmates) and for the President's antiterrorism bill signed in 1996. The antiterrorism bill placed limitations on habeas corpus under the Effective Death Penalty Act of 1996.

TURNER v. SAFELY REVISITED

The *Turner* decision is considered one of the most important cases in correctional law. Though the case examined issues concerning inmates' rights to receive and send mail and to get married, its ruling impacts almost every issue arising from correctional law and has far reaching impact on the correctional system. According to *Turner*, any prison regulation that is reasonably related to a legitimate penological interest will be held as valid, even if it violates an inmate's constitutional rights. While this case gives prison administrators the power and control over the smooth running of their correctional facility to promote order, security, and rehabilitation, it is considered a setback to inmates bringing litigation before the courts. The case virtually means that inmates cannot prevail against prison administrators once they justify a particular regulation or practice that a prisoner challenges. Though *Turner* was decided in 1987, the case is almost always cited in correctional law when inmates challenge practices of the institution that has custody over them.

A major concern that emerged with the prison legal rights revolution in the 1960s was that officials lost control of their facilities. Critics of the inmate rights movement contend that with an increase in prisoners' rights also came a rash of prison violence, riots, and insecurities among the inmate population, as well as others employed in the correctional system. However, they argue that *Turne*r gives penal administrators back the control they lost in the 1970s to effectively run their institutions. However, it does not give them the power or legal right to engage in abusive or freakish behavior, but rather it places security needs above the rights of inmates. In essence, *Turner* was a balancing test between the constitutional rights of the inmates and the needs of the prisons to sustain themselves. The Court decided that the needs of prison administrators to effectively execute their duties superceded the rights of prisoners to challenge regulations and even the conditions of their confinement.

The restrictions placed on inmates before they can file a Section 1983 claim, the decline in granting the writ of habeas corpus, and the *Turner* decision signal to many observers the direction in which the court is moving and the impact that these decisions will have on inmates' rights and correctional law. The Prison Litigation Reform Act of 1995, for example, has solely disarmed offenders seeking to file a Section 1983 claim. With the passage of the Act in 1996, inmates' claims must literally survive a process by which they can establish that a Section 1983 remedy is the most appropriate course of action. If the issue or matter can be resolved within the context of the penal setting, the complaint will be brought to an end and the matter will not advance to the federal court system. This Act was created to eliminate trivial and frivolous lawsuits with which inmates attempt to flood the courts. Furthermore, restrictions have been placed on inmates' opportunities to petition for a writ of habeas corpus. The *Turner* case makes it increasingly difficult for prisoners to prevail in cases regarding prison regulations and policies. If penal administrators can show that the regulation or policy is justified because it promotes security, order, and rehabilitation of the offenders, the regulation that the offender is contesting will be upheld by the court, even if such a regulation violates the constitutional rights of inmates. This precedent essentially gives penal administrators a green light to control their institutions in the manner they see fit provided they justify the reason they have regulations that prisoners find objectionable. Though the prison rights movement started in the 1960s and continued through the 1980s, many decisions made in the late 1980s and 1990s appear to adversely affect the fate of inmates. Though they retain many constitutional rights and safeguards that were uncommon to them prior to the 1960s, it appears that conservative decisions are rolling back the hands of time now that the federal courts are no longer receptive to judicial activism.

Key Terms

Effective Death Penalty Act of 1996
Prison Litigation Reform Act of 1995
Writ of Habeas Corpus

CASES CITED

Wainwright v. Sykes, 434 U.S. 880 (1977)
Turner v. Safley, 41 Cr.L. 3239 (1987)
Teague v. Lane, 109 S.Ct. 1060 (1989)

REFERENCES

Anderson, P. R., and Newman, D. J. (1993). Introduction to Criminal Justice. (5th ed.). New York: McGraw-Hill, Inc.

Cheurprakobkit, S., and Theis, J. (1999). The Decline of Habeas Corpus. The Justice Professional. 12(1): 3-16.

del Carmen, R.V., Ritter, S. E., and Witt, B.A. (1998). Briefs of Leading Cases in Corrections. (2ed.). Cincinnati, OH: Anderson Publishing Co.

Friedman, B. (1995). "Failed Enterprise: The Supreme Court's Habeas Corpus Reform," California Law Review. 83(2):485-546).

CHAPTER 11

The Future of Inmates' Rights and Litigations

FOCAL POINTS

- Composition of the Supreme Court
- AIDS and Geriatric Prisoners
- Privatization and Inmates
- Same Sex Marriages and Conjugal Visits
- DNA Testing and Prison Litigation
- Key Terms

Making predictions, especially for people in places of confinement, presents a formidable challenge to both criminal justice experts and legal scholars, for the law constantly changes to keep pace with a developing and evolving society. Change in the implementation and interpretation of the law is an inevitable consequence. Nevertheless, previously decided court rulings, cases, and Congressional acts may signal the direction in which correctional rights and litigations are headed.

A historical review reveals that the courts have basically experienced three periods of concern over prisoners' rights: (1) hands-off (pre-1960s); (2) hands-on, or judicial activism (post-1960s to the latter 1980s); and (3) hands-off (1987 to the present). However, it is important to note at this time that it is very unlikely that the courts will ever again return to a period of complete hands-off concerning the rights of prisoners. For such inaction to occur, the body of existing case law would either have to be ignored or overturned. Therefore, prisoners will retain some constitutional rights and entitlements as long as the Bill of Rights, and state and federal constitutions remain living documents. However, prisoners will not enjoy rights and entitlements to the extent that people in the free community do or to the extent that prevents penal administrators from maintaining the smooth functioning of order, security, and rehabilitative efforts of their correctional institutions.

Before making any predictions about what the future will hold for prisoners, it is important to chronicle the overall effects that the prisoners' rights movement has had on the state of corrections in America. Jacobs (1989) argues that the effects of judicial intervention helped the prisoners' rights movement to (1) contribute to the bureaucratization of the prison, (2) produce a new generation of administrators, (3) expand the procedural due process protections of prisoners, (4) make the general public aware of the conditions of confinement that prisoners had to endure, (5) create expectations among prisoners that they would have their concerns heard and be hopeful that reforms would be forthcoming, (6) demoralize prison administration and staff, (7) cause management and staff to lose control of prisoners and the institution, (8) create a movement to establish professional standards to be accepted and implemented by all correctional facilities, and (9) increase the creation of more prisons to reduce the problem of overcrowding.

Essentially, Jacobs believes that the prisoners' rights movement has been beneficial to inmates and adverse to prison administrators, staff, line officers, and the general public. On the one hand, the insufferable conditions of confinement to which inmates were once subjected have been ruled inhumane and corrected at the expense of increased taxpayer dollars. Some changes have resulted in the building of more facilities to reduce the number of inmates that can be housed at each facility. Furthermore, when consent decrees are forced upon prison administrators to make changes to their facilities, the money used to make changes comes from state legislatures that would rather use state funds to support education, road construction, or social programs in the free community to help law-abiding taxpayers. Prison officials have had to enter into consent decrees and contend with a court-appointed special master to ensure that changes in their facilities have been properly made so as to satisfy constitutional standards. On the other hand, the authority and power once exerted by prison officials and staff with impunity has been taken away, and in many cases ruled as either a show of deliberate indifference to the plight of prisoners or of a wanton and freakish nature that violates the cruel and usual punishment clause. Critics complain that with the newly found rights that prisoners won in court and the diminished power of prison officials came waves of inmate violence that threatened the safety and security of inmates, as well as prison officials, staff, and line officers.

Because of court intervention, inmates now enjoy procedural due process rights where they have a liberty interest. They are provided medical treatment though not state of the art. They can engage in their own religious practice. They can receive visitation and mail from friends, family, lawyers, and religious advisors. They must be provided a hearing before being placed into isolation for extended periods of time, before having "good time" credits taken away because of disciplinary action, or before being forced to take medication if they believe they do not need such treatment.

As a result of the hands-on approach, penal administrators must ensure that the number of staff and line officers is adequate to accommodate the number of prisoners, are properly trained, and know how the rule of law applies to each constitutionally-protected area that could range from the First to the Fourteenth Amendments. Such amendments protect freedom of the press, association (marriage), and the right to send and receive mail. These amendments also protect against cruel and unusual punishment, and the right to receive medical treatment. Furthermore, prisoners enjoy equal protections of the law and are afforded due process protections when there are liberty interests at stake. Moreover, prison administrators cannot rely on the usage of "elite" cons to essentially serve in the capacity of quasi-guards.

The conservative mood of the country in general, and the criminal justice system in particular, was widespread in the 1980s. During this time, the nation had already invoked its "get tough" stand against law violators. Experts contend that during this period efforts were made to reduce the number of crimes being committed. As a result, state legislatures passed and enacted laws advocating strict sentencing guidelines in the form of mandatory sentencing policies, "Three Strikes and You're Out," and a greater use of the death penalty for the commission of certain crimes. These conservative policies had the effect of adding to an already crowded prison system. The "get tough" approach reflected the mood of the country with respect to its views about how to better handle crime and criminals. Some legal scholars argued that the legal system was not immune from harnessing the same sentiments. They contend that the *Turner* case reflected the get tough policies of the 1980s.

Some corrections experts argue that excessive inmate litigation sparked the trend towards judicial nonintervention. For example, Howard (1982) reported that after *Copper* was decided in 1964, inmates filed 218 petitions by 1968. However, by 1981, inmates had filed more than 16,741 petitions. Similarly, Flanagan and Maguire (1992) reported that in 1980 state and federal inmates had filed 23,287 petitions alleging criminal and civil violations. In these claims, inmates sought compensatory, as well as injunctive, relief from the respective correctional facilities. Maguire and Pastore (1996) report that by 1990 the number of petitions reached 43,000 and increased to 64,000 by 1996. Despite this increase, Thomas (1996) argues that though the number of petitions filed in the early 1990s exceeded 40,000, 95 percent of them were found to be without merit, were dismissed, and never reached the preliminary trial stage. This clogging of the federal courts served to agitate the patience of federal judges, as well as prison administrators who had to answer many charges when claims made it to court.

The Prison Litigation Reform Act adversely affected prisoners' ability to file petitions and have their claims heard before federal courts. The Act placed restrictions on the number of cases an inmate could file in federal court and required that the inmate defray the cost of his own expenses. Though initiated in 1996, the number of Section 1983 lawsuits filed had plummeted by 90 percent the next year. This was seen as a major setback to the accomplishments of the prisoners' rights revolution, especially when compared to what had been occurring prior to the passage of this act when no limits were placed on the number of petitions a prisoner could file. Moreover, attorney fees were generously awarded. Many experts argue that such generosity may have led to the encouragement of frivolous lawsuits prisoners filed that consumed and flooded the federal courts' time and resources. As a reaction to the federal courts essentially closing the door on excessive inmate litigation, prisoners began filing their claims in state courts. The state courts, in turn, began adopting laws similar to those enacted by the federal courts. The outcome has been an erosion of prison litigation and judicial activism.

Composition of the Supreme Court

History indicates that the composition of the Supreme Court has consistently guided how it goes about deciding cases. For example, the Warren Court, mainly composed of liberals, decided a series of cases that became landmarks because they advocated civil liberties and constitutional safeguards and protections of its citizens. However, the Burger and Rehnquist Courts almost always rendered conservative decisions and have gone so far as to overturn many of the rulings of the Warren Court. During the 1980s, when *Turner* was decided, the composition of the court was mainly conservative. Therefore, as long as the composition remains conservative, it stands to reason that the overwhelming majority of the Supreme Court's decisions will reflect its conservative views, and thereby have an adverse impact on prisoners' rights in the future.

AIDS and Geriatric Prisoners

One area of future litigation will involve adequate medical care to AIDS and geriatric prisoners. While *Estelle v. Gamble* essentially declared that the holding state must provide the prisoner with medical care because he cannot secure it for himself by virtue of his imprisonment, it does not provide for state of the art medical treatment. The need for medical treatment could prove to be very litigious in the future, since there is a growing population of HIV/AIDS and elderly prisoners. These "special needs" inmates will naturally require more medical attention than other prisoners. Since medical treatment can be very expensive, this begs the question, to what extent are correctional officials legally responsible for providing expensive treatment and medication over extended periods of time? The courts have not addressed this issue. For example, correctional agencies report that two of the most expensive special needs groups to keep confined are inmates with acquired immune deficiency syndrome (AIDS) and geriatric inmates. These groups are the most expensive, because elderly inmates require constant medication and expensive surgery, and treating inmates with AIDS costs correctional facilities $50,000 yearly per inmate. It is estimated that there are nearly 80,000 inmates infected with the AIDS virus (Cauchon, 1995). This estimate could mean great economic hardship if the AIDS virus continues to spread at the current rate in places of confinement, since there is no sign that a cure for this disease is anywhere in sight.

Privatization and Inmates

Another area of future prison litigation will invariably lead to a discussion of the privatization of prisons. Because of the growing number of states that are moving towards privatizing corrections, experts believe that this will be a hotly litigated area. Privatization is the process by which private individuals and corporations, become involved in the management and operations of correctional institutions (Adler, Mueller, and Laufer, 1994). They are non-governmental entities. Therefore, ownership is delegated to private individuals and corporations because it is believed to be an economically profitable way to run such prisons. Though there are a host of questions levied against such prisons (mainly security and custody), perhaps the biggest question asked of privatization is, can the sovereign right of the people to punish and discipline inmates be transferred to private individuals who manage and operate correctional facilities? Stated another way, can non-governmental entities be given the authority to deprive prisoners of their liberty interest? For example, state and federal correctional facilities are governed by the Fifth and

Fourteenth Amendments to not deny prisoners life, liberty, or property without due process of law. To what extent does this constitutional safeguard and protection apply to non-governmental personnel or entities? Moreover, if an inmate confined in a private prison alleges that private correctional guards destroyed or took property from his cell valued at a hundred dollars, or subjected him to excessive force, how would he get his claim resolved or heard? Where can he find a remedy? Can he invoke a Section 1983 lawsuit or seek redress in a state tort claim?

Private prisons also raise other salient questions that could be the subject of future litigations. Though private prisons exist to maximize profits, are they legally responsible for providing HIV/AIDS prisoners or others in their custody with medical treatment whenever the occasion arises? Granted that in many cases private prisons will almost always elect to house non-threatening, low-risk offenders, it may be more difficult selecting inmates who do not appear to have a medical condition. Take the example of people infected with the AIDS virus. Sometimes, it is possible to be infected and not show any physical symptoms that might indicate to others that one suffers from the disease, have a need for medical treatment, or be a potential medical liability to whomever is responsible for providing treatment. Other questions may include the following: Can private entities award or remove "good time" to and from prisoners? Are they responsible for injuries or the death of people in the free community caused by escaped prisoners? Are they responsible for capturing such fugitives? Can they discipline inmates and even place them in isolation? Can they transfer prisoners to a state or federal prison without providing them due process? Can private corporations arbitrarily increase the costs of incarcerating prisoners? These are only a few questions that appear to be inevitable legal issues concerning private prisons.

Experts contend that prison litigation can be substantially reduced if prisons and jails are made humane. (If they are not, experts warn that courts may again be willing to intervene on behalf of prisoners and hear complaints). One viable strategy that can be used by states to operate their prisons is to create a national standard that meets constitutional muster and provides safeguards and protection to prisoners. These standards should be proposed by the American Correctional Association (ACA). ACA should create a body of criteria in the form of a written policy that addresses all aspects of an inmate's confinement that includes such areas as (a) searches of inmates, as well as their cell, (b) the sanitary and proper means to prepare food, (c) the number of showers inmates are to be allowed, and (d) the use of sensor devices to conduct body cavity searches instead of dehumanizing practices (Robin, 1986) to only name a few. ACA could award accreditation status to facilities that meet their guidelines and policies. Receiving accreditation could signal to judges and juries that penal administrators are not operating in a manner that is deliberately indifferent to the needs of inmates.

Same Sex Marriages and Conjugal Visits

If history is a good indicator, it is very likely that future prison litigation will have to address the issue of same sex marriages and conjugal visits. Though conjugal visits are left to the complete discretion of the penal administrators, such visitation policies could be challenged on the premise that they violate the equal protection clause that mandates that all inmates should be treated equally and not be subjected to disparate treatment. Recently, the state government of Vermont agreed to allow same sex, or homosexual, marriages. If this trend catches on in other states and spills over into the prison setting similar to other trends (e.g. the civil rights movement resulting in the prisoners' rights movement), it is possible that the courts will have to address this issue. It is widely known that homosexual practices are commonplace in places of confinement. Therefore, it stands to reason that this could be a litigated issue in the future, especially in prisons found in Vermont and Hawaii where the free community has accepted same sex marriages. Conjugal visits are only allowed in some states where inmates can show proof that they are married. If homosexuals are allowed to marry, prison administrators would be hard pressed not to allow conjugal visitation to spouses. Any policies prohibiting conjugal visits based on same sex marriages would demonstrate an obvious denial of equal protection under the law.

DNA Testing and Prison Litigation

The prospect of DNA testing raises other question that could be the subject of future inmate litigation. DNA (deoxyribonucleic acid) is the hereditary material that is passed from parent to child. The combination of parental DNA sequence gives each offspring a unique genetic profile. DNA is composed of the deoxyribonucleic acids (commonly referred to as bases) adenine (A), thymine (T), cytosine (C) and guanine (G). A strand of DNA is composed of the nucleic acid bases bound to each other in any number of combinations forming a "ribbon-like" structure that is known as single stranded DNA. Two "ribbons" of DNA (or an individual base) can bind to each other if, and only if, they contain complimentary sequences. The A bases compliment with Ts and Cs compliment Gs. These complexes form what is known as double stranded DNA.

The function of DNA is to allow a person's cells to make the materials it needs to survive. DNA contains the sequence of genes that direct individual characteristics from a person's hair color to the enzymes that break down fat. Gene expression is directed by signals that respond to a person's environment or situation. For example, eating food triggers the synthesis of certain proteins that aid in the transport and digestion of nutrients. The process of protein synthesis occurs by a logical sequence of events starting with the copying of a particular DNA sequence into ribonucleic acid (RNA). This process is called RNA transcription. Directed by other cellular signals, the RNA is converted to protein (transcription). RNA consists of a modified form of DNA and consists of the bases A, C, G, and U (uracil). Each set of four ribonucleic acid bases codes for each of the 20 basic amino acids. For example, the RNA base combination of CUU codes for the amino acid Luecine while CCU codes for the amino acid Proline. This coding scheme allows a large amount of information to be translated into endless combinations of proteins sequences. The proteins are finally processed by organelles (mini organs in each cell that put the finishing touches on proteins) or other enzymes and are now ready to perform their function.

Recent scientific advances have made the analysis of DNA a precise tool for identifying individuals from a small amount of genetic material. Genetic material are objects originating from a person's body that contains cells with a nucleus. The genetic material that is commonly used for genetic analysis includes hair, blood samples, body tissue, teeth, bones and saliva. DNA is removed from these samples and subjected to a variety of tests, including the analysis of tandemly-repeated DNA and restriction fragment length polymorphisms (RFLP). The DNA of each individual contains a variety of loci (locations or specific regions). Some loci are used as templates to make protein and some are not. Among the sequences that are not destined to become proteins are short sequences that are repeated several times. These repeats are called tandem repeats and may be arranged in small (minisatellites) or large (microsatellites) groups. The number of repeats varies from person to person. Therefore, if one were to cut DNA into pieces at specific sites (restriction enzyme digestion), the size of these pieces would be different from person to person depending on the number of repeats that an individual's DNA contains. This digestion reveals a unique DNA profile.

Another approach to analyzing tandemly repeated DNA includes the technique of the polymerase chain reaction, or PCR. PCR allows the use of minute quantities of genetic material. In this procedure, DNA primers bind to specific DNA sequences when the DNA "ribbons" are separated using high temperatures (around 90C). A primer is a DNA sequence that is complimentary to some other known sequence (remember A binds to T and C binds to G). This primer then binds to one strand of the ribbon when the temperature is lowered. A thermophillic enzyme (an enzyme that functions at temperatures exceeding 90°C) and individual bases are included in the reaction mix and when the temperature is raised around 70°C, the bases are incorporated into a new ribbon of DNA. The process allows the identification of specific regions of DNA that contain varying numbers of repeated DNA and reveals the different lengths of DNA, thus revealing a unique profile.

RFLP, on the other hand, looks at the differences in individual base pairs by using restriction enzymes to reveal sequence differences that are normally present in each person's DNA. For example, if person A contains the DNA sequence AGACTT, there are no known enzymes that specifically cut DNA in this region. On the other hand, if person B has the DNA sequence GGACTT, it can be cut by the restriction enzyme BamHI. As a result, this region in person A will be seen as a long piece of DNA whereas in person B, it will be seen as two shorter pieces of DNA.

In light of the recent O.J. Simpson trial that captured the attention of the nation, defense attorney Barry Scheck introduced the viewing audience to the strengths and weaknesses associated with DNA evidence. He revealed that DNA testing can be used to isolate a single offender from billions of other suspects if the evidence is properly handled and is not contaminated before DNA testing begins. He also argued that if crime scene investigators, or the crime lab, mishandle evidence by contaminating it, any findings discovered are not conclusive and are suspect at best.

Recently, many inmates (especially those accused and convicted of rape) have been released and exonerated after DNA testing revealed their innocence and that they had been falsely accused, even in some cases where eye witnesses testified against the defendant. Though there are many prisoners who have maintained their innocence since being arrested (some honest and others dishonest), the courts may be faced with the prospect of having to review many cases in light of DNA testing. DNA is unique in that no two people share similar genetic codes. However, the exception can be found in monozygotic (identical) twins. Therefore, DNA evidence collected at a crime scene can be used to connect a suspect to, or exclude him or her from, having committed a particular crime.

Key Terms

conjugal visits
DNA
geriatric prisoners
privatization

RNA

CASE CITED

Estelle v. Gamble, 429 U.S. 465 (1976)

REFERENCES

Adler, F., Mueller, G.O., and Laufer, W.S. (1994). Criminal Justice. New York: McGraw-Hill.

Cauchon, D. (1995). "AIDS in Prison: Locked Up and Locked Out." *USA Today*, March 31, 1995:6A.

Cripe, C. A. (1997). Legal Aspects of Corrections Management. Gaithersburg, MD: Aspen Publication.

Flanagan, T.J., and Maguire, K. (1992). (Eds.). Sourcebook of Criminal Justice Statistics 1991. US Department of Justice, Bureau of Justice Statistics (Washington, D.C.: U.S. Government Printing Office), p.555.

Howard, A.E.D. (1982). "The States and the Supreme Court," 31 Catholic University Law Review. 375, at 379.

Jacobs, J. B. (1989). "The Prisoners Rights Movement." in The American Prisons: Issues in Research and Policy (Eds.). Alfred Blumstein. New York: Plenum Press.

Maguire, K., and Pastore, A. L. (1996). (Eds.). Sourcebook of Criminal Justice Statistics 1995. US Department of Justice, Bureau of Justice Statistics (Washington, D.C.: U.S. Government Printing Office), p.177.

Robin, G.D. (1986). Introduction to the Criminal Justice System. 3rd ed. New York: Harper and Row Publishers.

Thomas, A.P. (1996). "Rule of Law: Congress Evokes Prisoners' Access to Frivolous Appeals." *Wall Street Journal*, July 3, A11.

APPENDIX

The Bill of Rights and the Fourteenth Amendment to the U.S. Constitution

FIRST AMENDMENT (ratified in 1791)

Congress shall make no law respecting an establishment of religion, or prohibiting the free exercise thereof; or abridging the freedom of speech, or of the press; or the right of the people peaceably to assemble, and to petition the Government for a redress of grievances.

SECOND AMENDMENT (ratified in 1791)

A well regulated Militia, being necessary for the security of a free State, the right of the people to keep and bear Arms, shall not be infringed.

THIRD AMENDMENT (ratified in 1791)

No Soldier shall, in time of peace be quartered in any house, without the consent of the Owner, nor in time of war, but in a manner to be prescribed by law.

FOURTH AMENDMENT (ratified in 1791)

The right of the people to be secure in their persons, houses, papers, and effects, against unreasonable searches and seizures, shall not be violated, and no Warrants shall issue, but upon probable cause, supported by Oath or affirmation, and particularly describing the place to be searched, and the persons or things to be seized.

FIFTH AMENDMENT (ratified in 1791)

No person shall be held to answer for a capital or otherwise infamous crime, unless on a presentment of indictment of a Grand Jury, except in cases arising in the land or naval forces, or in the Militia, when in actual service in time of War or public danger; nor shall any person be subject for the same offence to be twice put in jeopardy of life or limb; nor shall be compelled in any criminal case to be a witness against himself, nor be deprived of life, liberty, or property, without due process of law; nor shall private property be taken for public use, without just compensation.

SIXTH AMENDMENT (ratified in 1791)

In all criminal prosecutions, the accused shall enjoy the right to a speedy and public trial, by an impartial jury of the State and district wherein the crime shall have been committed, which district shall have been previously ascertained by law, and to be informed of the nature and cause of the accusation; to be confronted with the witnesses against him; to have compulsory process for obtaining witnesses in his favor, and to have the Assistance of Counsel for his defense.

SEVENTH AMENDMENT (ratified in 1791)

In Suits at law, where the value in controversy shall exceed twenty dollars, the right of trial by jury shall be preserved, and no fact tried by a jury, shall be otherwise re-examined in any Court of the United States, than according to the rules of the common law.

EIGHTH AMENDMENT (ratified in 1791)

Excessive bail shall not be required, nor excessive fines imposed, nor cruel and unusual punishment inflicted.

NINTH AMENDMENT (ratified in 1791)

The enumeration in the Constitution, or certain rights, shall not be construed to deny or disparage others retained by the people.

TENTH AMENDMENT (ratified in 1791)

The powers not delegated to the United States by the Constitution, nor prohibited by it to the States, are reserved to the States respectively, or to the people.

FOURTEENTH AMENDMENT (ratified in 1868):

Section 1. All persons born or naturalized in the United States, and subject to the jurisdiction thereof, are citizens of the United States and of the States wherein they reside. No State shall make or enforce any law which shall abridge the privileges or immunities of citizens of the United States; nor shall any State deprive any person of life, liberty, or property without due process of law; nor deny to any person within its jurisdiction the equal protection of the laws....

Section 5. The Congress shall have the power to enforce, by appropriate legislation, the provisions of this article.

TABLE of CASES

FIRST AMENDMENT

Fulwood v. Clemmer, 206 F. Supp. 370 (D.D.C.) (1962)
Johnson v. Avery, 393 U.S. 483 (1969)
Bell v. Wolfish, 441 U.S. 520 (1979)
Gittlemacker v. Prosse, 428 F.2d (3rd Cir. 1970)
Bounds v. Smith, 430 U.S. 817 (1977)
Cruz v. Beto, 405 U.S. 319 (1972)
Goring v. Aaron, 350 F. Supp. 1 (D. Minn. 1972)
Theriault v. Carlson, 339 F. Supp. 375 (N.D. Ga. 1973)
Lyon v. Gilligan, 382 F. Supp. 198 (N.D. Ohio, 1974)
Pell v. Procunier, 417 U.S. 817 (1974)
Procunier v. Martinez, 416 U.S. 396 (1974)
Saxbe v. Washington Post, 417 U.S. 843 (1974)
Kahane v. Carlson, 527 F. 2d 592 (2d Cir.) (1975)
Theriault v. Silber, 391 F. Supp. 578 (W.D. Tex. 1975)
Garrett v. Estelle, 536 F.2d 1274 (5th Cir. 1977)
Jones v. North Carolina Prisoners' Labor Union, Inc., 433 U.S. 119 (1977)
Moskowitz v. Wilkinson, 432 F. Supp. 947 (D. Conn. 1977)
Houchins v. KQED, Inc. 438 U.S. 1 (1978)
Moore v. Carlson, Civil No. 77-982, M.D. Pa., 1978
Procunier v. Navarette, 434 U.S. 555 (1978)
Jones v. Bradley, 590 F.2d 294 (9th Cir. 1979)
Block v. Rutherford, 468 U.S. 576 (1984)
Brown v. Johnson, 743 F.2d 405 (6th Cir. 1984)
Mary of Oakknull v. Coughlin, 475 N.Y.S. 644 (N.4. App. Div. 1984)
Robert v. U.S. Jaycees, 464 U.S. 609 (1984)
Smith v. Coughlin, 748 F.2d 783 (1984)
Thongvanh v. Thalacker, 17 F.3d. (1994)
Udey v. Kastner, 805 F.2d (5th Cir.) 1986
O'Lane v. Estate of Shabazz, 41 Cr.L. 3251 (1987)
Turner v. Safley, 41 Cr.L. 3239 (1987)
Pollock v. Marshall, 845 F.2d 656 (6th Cir. 1988)
Benjamin v. Caughlin, 708 F. Supp. 570 (S.D.N.Y.) (1989)
Kentucky Department of Corrections v. Thompson, 490 U.S. 454, 109 S.Ct. 1904 (1989)
McCorkle v. Johnson, 881 F.2d 993 (11th Cir. 1989)
Murray v. Giarrantano, 109 S.Ct. 2765 (1989)
Thornburgh v. Abbott, 490 U.S. (1989)
Cromwell v. Coughlin, 773 F. Supp. 606 (S.D.N.Y 1991)
Giano v. Senkowski, 54 F. 3rd 1050 (2d Cir. 1995)

Lewis v. Casey, 64 L.W. 4587 (1996)

FOURTH AMENDMENT

Lanza v. New York, 370 U.S. 139 (1962)
Goff v. Nix, 803 F.2d States v. Hitchcock, 467 F.2d 1107 (1972)
Stone v. Powell 358 (8th Cir. 1968)
United, 428 U.S. 465 (1976)
United States v. Hearst, 563 F.2d 1331 (9th Cir. 1977)
Bell v. Wolfish, 441 U.S. 520 (1979)
Forts v. Ward, 621 F.2d 1210 (2d Cir. 1980)
Lee v. Downs, 641 F.2d 1117 (4th Cir. 1981)
Block v. Rutherford, 468 U.S. 576 (1984)
Hudson v. Palmer, 35 Cr.L. 3230 (1984)
Dunn v. White, 45 Cr.L. 2360 (1989)
Watson v. Jones, 980 F.2d 1165 (8th Cir. 1992)
Jordan v. Gardner, 986 F.2d 1521 (9th Cir. 1993)

EIGHTH AMENDMENT

Talley v. Stephens, 247 F. Supp. 683 (E.D. Ark.) (1965)
Jackson v. Bishop, 404 F.2d 371 (8th Cir. 1068) (1968)
Holt v. Sarver, 300 F. Supp. 825 (E.D. Ark.) (1970)
Furman v. Georgia, 408 U.S. 238 (1972)
Logue v. United States, 412 U.S. 521 (1973)
Estelle v. Gamble, 429 U.S. 465 (1976)
Gregg v. Georgia, 428 U.S. 153 (1976)
Hutto v. Finney, 437 U.S. 678 (1978)
Ruiz v. Estelle, 503 F. Supp. 1265 S.D. Tex. (1980)
Rhodes v. Chapman, 452 U.S. 337 (1981)
City of Revere v. Massachusetts General Hospital, 463 U.S. 239 (1983)
Smith v. Wade, 33 Cr.L. 3021 (1983)
Whitley v. Albers, 475 U.S. 312 (1986)
Doe v. Couglin, (D.C.N.Y. No. 88-CV-964) (1988)
Roe v. Fauver, 43 Cr.L. 2174 (1988)
West v. Atkins, 108 S.Ct. 2250 (1988)
Wood v. White, 689 F. Supp. 874 (W.D. Wis. 1988)
Washington v. Harper, 58 L.W. 4249 (1990)
Harris v. Thigpen, 941 F.2d 1495 (11th Cir. 1991)
Wilson v. Seiter, 501 U.S. 294 (1991)
Heflin v. Stewart County, 958 F.2d 709 (6th Cir. 1992)
Hudson v. McMillian, 60 L.W. 4151 (1992)

Blumhagen v. Sabes, 834 F. Supp. 1347 (D.Wyo. 1993)
Helling v. Mc Kinney, 53 Cr.L. 2230 (1993)
Reed v. Woodruff County, 7 F.3d 808 (8th Cir. 1993)
Farmer v. Brennan, 55 Cr.L. 2135 (1994)
Myers v. Lake County, 30 F.3d 847 (7th Cir. 1994)
Gates v. Rowland, 39 F.3d 1439 (9th Cir. 1995)
Jolly v. Coughlin, 894 F. Supp. 734 (S.D.N.Y. 1995)

FOURTEENTH AMENDMENT

Lee v. Washington, 390 U.S. 333 (1968)
Wolff v. McDonnell, 418 U.S. 539 (1974)
Baxter v. Palmigiano, 425 U.S. 308 (1976)
Meachum v. Fano, 427 U.S. 215 (1976)
Montanye v. Haymes, 427 U.S. 236 (1976)
Rosada v. Civiletti, 621 F.2d 1179 (2d Cir. 1980)
United States v. Bailey, 40.78-990 (1980)
Vitek v. Jones, 445 U.S. 480 (1980)
Howe v. Smith, 452 U.S. 473 (1981)
Parratt v. Taylor, 451 U.S. 527 (1981)
Hewitt v. Helms, 459 U.S. 460 (1983)
Olim v. Wakinekona, 416 U.S. 238 (1983)
Hudson v. Palmer, 468 U.S. 517 (1984)
United States v. Gouveia, 467 U.S. 180 (1984)
Cleavinger v. Saxner, 106 S.Ct. 496 (1985)
Ponte v. Real, 37 Cr.L. 3051 (1985)
Superintendent v. Hill, 472 U.S. 445 (1985)
Daniel v. Williams, 474 U.S. 327 (1986)
Davidson v. Cannon, 474 U.S. 344 (1986)
Muhammad v. Carlson, 43 Cr.L. 2131 (1988)
Marquez Ramon v. Reno, 69 F.3d 477 (10th Cir. 1995)
Sandin v. Conner, 115 S.Ct. 2293 (1995)

GLOSSARY

absolute certainty A level of evidence that is not required in any criminal or civil case

absolute immunity Complete protection from civil lawsuits enjoyed by the U.S. president, judges, and prosecutors for official decisions they make.

access to the courts Fundamental prisoner's right that is the key element for enforcement of other rights because it is the mechanism for gaining judicial protection of constitutional rights. This right includes protected contacts with lawyers and provision of legal resources for case preparation.

acquit To relieve from a charge of fault or crime.

actus reus One of the elements that must be established before one can be found guilty of committing a crime. It is the wrongful deed or the unlawful act. It must be proven along with mens rea (guilty mind).

American Civil Liberties Union (ACLU) An organization that is charged with guaranteeing the civil rights of people charged with committing a crime or persons who have been wronged by the American government.

appellate court A court that does not retry a case but rather reviews the procedures to determine if the lower court erred in its interpretation of the law or excluded evidence that should have been included. The courts are found on the state and federal levels. State appeals court are called state courts of appeal. On the federal level, these courts are called U.S. District Courts and the U.S. Supreme Court.

Article III, Section I of the U.S. Constitution The judicial power of the United States shall be vested in one Supreme Court and in such inferior courts as the Congress, may from time to time, ordain and establish.

Article IX of the U.S. Constitution The right to a writ of habeas corpus is found in Article 9.

attorney fees Part of an award paid to attorneys who prevail in Section 1983 litigations.

bill of indictment A formal written accusation from the grand jury presented to the court for prosecution against the accused person.

bill of information A document granted by a judge after an accusation by the prosecutor that a crime has been committed showing a finding of probable cause to believe that a suspect has committed a crime and the matter should go to trial. It is issued in states and jurisdiction that do not rely on the grand jury system.

Bill of Rights Typically refers to the first ten amendments in the Constitution that set forth certain freedoms and guarantees to U.S. citizens.

body cavity search A strip search that includes examinations of bodily openings that might be used to hide contraband after contact visits. The Supreme Court has approved such searches, even for non-convicted pretrial detainees, because of concerns about safety and security within jails and other detention facilities.

change of venue A request that a trial take place in another location, since it is believed that the accused will not receive a fair and impartial trial in a particular location.

class action In civil law, a group or collective of injured persons join together in one legal action. It refers to a lawsuit on behalf of a segment of the population that has sustained similar damage or injury.

clear and convincing evidence That which indicates that the thing to be proved is highly probable or reasonably certain. Its burden of proof is greater than that of the preponderance of evidence but less than that required to establish guilt beyond a reasonable doubt.

civil law The branch of the law that deals with contracts and personal injuries or damages. It is state and federal law pertaining to noncriminal activities. A body of formal rules created by a society for self regulation.

civil liberties Rights that are guaranteed by the U.S. Constitution and the Bill of Rights.

Civil Rights Act of 1871 Referred to as Section 1983, states that any person acting under color of law who violates the Constitutional or federally protected rights of a citizen of the United States will be held liable. It may also pertain to civil suits filed by employers against their employers where discrimination has occurred. It is found within Title 42 Section 1983 of the United States Code.

Civil Rights of Institutionalized Persons Act A federal law setting standards for grievance procedures in state correctional institutions.

Civil Rights Movement The social, political, and economic struggles for equality by people locked out of the mainstream. The movement started in the 50s and continued into the mid 1970s. Those who participated in the movement were demanding due process and equal protection under the law.

color of law Officials working in the capacity as officers representing the law and legal authority or acting in one's official capacity typically as a law enforcement officer or agent of the justice system. It also refers to customs of the people.

common law The legal system that the United States inherited from England in which judges create law by deciding cases while relying on judges' opinions in prior similar cases.

compensatory damages In civil law those who are injured because of the actions of others or of a corporation typically ask for a monetary sum to defray or compensate for the cost of the injury they sustained.

complaint The initial filing in a civil lawsuit that presents allegations about the defendant's legal responsibility for harms suffered by the claimant.

concurring opinion The opinion by an appellate judge who agrees with the outcome of case but disagrees with some aspect of the reasoning in the majority opinion.

conditions of parole Specified rules and regulations that must be adhered to in order for the offender to remain eligible for release after serving time in a correctional facility. When conditions are violated such as the commission of a crime or a technical violation of a guideline, the offender could be resentenced to prison.

conditions of probation Specified rules and regulations that must be adhered to in order for the offender to remain eligible to remain in the community. Probation is normally given to offenders who have not been incarcerated and is a legal status from a court.

conflict model A criminal justice paradigm that argues that the subcomponents in the system do not work together to reach a common goal and instead subcomponents have their own agendas.

conjugal visits A visit by a spouse or friend that allows for physical or sexual contact. In most states, prison officials require that inmates show proof of marriage. For these meetings, an appropriate setting is used to secure privacy.

consensus model A criminal justice paradigm that argues that every element or subcomponent in the system work together for the goal of delivering fair and evenhanded justice to everyone.

consent decree A negotiated resolution to a prison reform lawsuit that becomes law as the order is issued by the judge. When consent decrees are entered into, the court they become the supervisor of the prison until the agreed upon changes are implemented. A failure to make the changes could mean that the prison could be shut down or an administrator could be fined or even sentenced to prison for failure to comply to the court order.

Constitution The fundamental laws contained in state or federal documents that outline the design of the government and the basic rights for individuals. It prescribes the structure or organization and major duties of the legislative, executive, and judicial branches of the government. It allocates power between the respective branches of government. It places restrictions on the exercise of that power, specifying what government may not do.

constitutional rights Legal guarantees, specified in the fundamental legal documents of a state or nation, to protect individuals against improper actions by government. Guarantees can be found in the U.S. Constitution and its Amendments.

contraband An item, such as a weapon, drugs, or money that prisoners are not allowed to possess and that officials seek to discover and seize in searches and mail inspections. Contraband is that which serves to negate the purpose of imprisonment by undermining security, safety, and rehabilitation.

contract law The part of the law that governs agreement between parties. Parties can be individuals, companies and corporation. Any disagreement between parties could result in litigation from other parties that are involved.

corporal punishment The use of physical punishment, most commonly recognized as beating and other pain-inflicting punishments, but also including restricted, uncomfortable confinement in a small space.

court of last resort The highest court in a judicial system, either a state supreme court or the U.S. Supreme Court. The court with the final say in matters of controversies. They are typically courts that receive an appeal from a defendant or petitioner.

courts of general jurisdiction These courts typically address matters concerning the commission of felony crimes and some civil actions. Criminal courts with the authority to hear all cases and in some states hear appeals from lower courts.

courts of limited jurisdiction Courts with only the authority to hear minor offenses or misdemeanor cases. These courts also have authority to try probable cause hearings in felony cases and sometimes felony trials that may result in penalties below a certain amount.

courts of special jurisdiction Typically these include family, juvenile, and probate courts.

criminal law A body of law that defines the procedural as well as the substantive criminal code. This body of law defines criminal offenses and prescribes punishment.

defendant A person who is facing a criminal procedure. A person about whom a grand jury or judge has found that probable cause exists to believe that he or she committed a crime and therefore must answer to the charges.

deliberate indifference A complete disregard for the welfare of the person in custody where assistance is need. Assistance could range from medical care to protection against physical violence directed at the person in custody. It is used as a standard by the court to determine if liability exists. The claim is usually raised in Eighth Amendment cases.

discretion The authority of corrections officials to make decisions based on their own judgement and not mandated or controlled by specific rules.

dissenting opinion The judicial opinion by an appellate judge who disagrees completely and does not concur with the court majority's decision on the outcome of a case.

district court Typically referred to as a federal trial court with general and original jurisdiction. Its jurisdiction may include several states or counties.

diversion A correctional strategy used to give an offender a reprieve by sentencing him or her to a community-based intermediate sanction instead of a traditional place of confinement (jails and prisons).

DNA The abbreviation for deoxyribonucleic acid. DNA is one of the two nucleic acids found in all cells.

double ceiling Also referred to as double bunking. Deals with placing two or more inmates in a jail or prison cell that was designed to accommodate only one prisoner.

due process of law A flexibly interpreted right contained in the Fifth and Fourteenth Amendments to the Constitution that is used to examine jail conditions for pretrial detainees, because the Eighth Amendment protects only convicted offenders, and not detainees who have not been convicted.

Eighth Amendment This amendment prohibits excessive bail and cruel and usual punishment. In corrections, the Eighth Amendment protects the prisoner or petitioner from practices that are considered to be in violation of contemporary standards of decency.

elite prisoners Convicts who are given special privilege and status by institutional authority. These prisoners serve as informants and help correctional guards run and operate prisons in an orderly manner. There have been numerous complaints about the brutality that elite cons have inflicted on other inmates. Elite convicts were used in most cases when the correctional facility did not have enough civilian correctional guards.

equal protection The right not to be discriminated against, guaranteed by the Fifth and Fourteenth Amendments and sometimes raised when prisoners from one religion believe they are being treated differently than prisoners from another religion. The Equal Protection Clause of the Constitution essentially states that all citizens must be treated the same unless there is a compelling reason that justifies differential treatment.

establishment clause The portion of the First Amendment that prevents government support or endorsement of particular religions. In essence, Congress or the state cannot create or establish a religion and require everyone to participate in that religion.

Federal Appeals Court These courts review cases that were already tried in the U.S. District Courts. They do not serve to provide a new trial but rather review cases that were tried on the lower level in the federal court system. These courts include U.S. Circuit Courts and the U.S. Supreme

Court.

federal trial court Referred to as a U.S. District court. Trial courts at the state or federal level with general and original jurisdiction.

felony A serious crime that carries a punishment of more than a year in prison, fine, probation, or a combination. Actions that are considered to be a serious offense against the state or people.

First Amendment This amendment guarantees freedom of speech, religion, press, the right to petition the government for a redress of grievances. It is considered one of the preferred amendments and carries the highest degree of protection.

Fourth Amendment This amendment prohibits unreasonable searches and seizures. The amendment applies to places where there is a reasonable expectation of privacy.

Fourteenth Amendment This amendment contains the equal protection and due process clauses that are applicable to the state government. It is normally incorporated into the Bill of Rights. This amendment sometimes require that a procedure follows when life, liberty, or property is in jeopardy.

free exercise clause That portion of the First Amendment that forbids government interference with people's religious beliefs and practices. The First Amendment guarantees to each individual the right to engage in the free exercise of one's religious beliefs and practices.

geriatric prisoners The term refers to a growing population of older inmates between the ages of 55 and 70. They are those who have aged out of crime and longer pose a threat to society. These inmates are viewed as an economic burden to places of incarceration because as they get older, they begin to experience declining health that the state must pay to treat.

good faith exception A legal defense used by a warden or prison administrator for violating an inmate's right. The defense means that the official thought that he or she was operating within the parameter of official policy. However, if there is no showing of good faith, the court may find that the official was acting in bad faith and rule in favor of the defendant or petitioner.

habeas corpus petition A petition filed by an offender who has been unsuccessful in the appellate process but who wishes to allege that his or her federal constitutional rights were violated during the investigation and prosecution of a criminal case. This petition permits a federal judge to review prior actions and decisions in state criminal cases. Used often by death row inmates.

hands-off policy The usual approach of judges to prisoners' rights cases prior to the 1960s because of a widespread belief that prisoners had no rights and that corrections officials were best qualified to run their own prisons and programs without interference. The hands-off policy may have been used because of an earlier case ruling that stated that prisoners were essentially slaves of the state with no rights.

incapacitation The process by which an offender is institutionalized for committing a crime. Offenders are confined when they pose a threat to the order and maintenance of society.

incorporation The process by which the U.S. Supreme Court applies provisions of the Bill of Rights to state and local governments by including them in the due process clause of the Fourteenth Amendment.

individual rights Procedural safeguards and constitutional entitlements afforded to suspects who face criminal prosecution.

injunctive relief A command to either end or desist a practice or to have one activated. In many petitions to the courts, prisoners typically request such remedies.

intentional torts These actions are filed when it can be shown that there is intention on the part of the officer to bring physical or psychological harm to someone. The burden of proof falls on the defendant or petitioner to show that the officer or official had the state of mind to intentionally harm.

intermediate sanctions Referred to as alternative to or diversions from a traditional sentence of imprisonment. Intermediate sanctions are reserved for first time offenders who have not committed a crime so serious as to mandate being placed in prison but whose crime cannot go unpunished. They are given a diversion as a reprieve. They are programs designed to reduce expensive prison cost, free needed bed space for harden criminals, and give nonviolent offenders a second chance to be law abiding.

issues The question of law or procedure being addressed by an court in a legal case. It is the legal fact to be decided by the court.

judicial activism The claim that certain judges make decisions exceeding proper judicial authority and thereby assume power that belongs to another branch of government, particularly the executive branch.

judicial review The power of U.S. judges to review actions by other branches of government to determine if those actions should be invalidated for violating constitutional law. The power of judicial review was initially established in *Marbury v. Madison* under the headship of Chief Justice John Marshall.

jurisdiction The legal issues and territory under the authority of a court in a city, county, state, or country.

jurisprudence A body or a system of laws that regulate all aspects of life.

level of proof The standard of evidence that needs to be established in a legal proceeding. Standards vary in criminal, civil and other legal matters.

mandamus relief See of Writ of Mandamus.

maximum security prison Prisons where inmates are subjected to the highest degree of custody and security. These inmates are segregated from each other and have restricted visitation. The level of security of each prison is determined by its physical composition and the classification of its prisoners.

medical treatment Care given to victims who have sustained treatable injuries and illnesses. Injuries may include cuts, broken or fractured bones, gunshots wounds, illnesses and others. Treatment is normally given by those trained in medicine. They are typically doctors, nurses, medics, or medical assistance certified with the knowledge of providing care to those who have taken ill or have sustain injuries that are either self-inflicted or caused by an external object or force. Only medical doctors are legally allowed to prescribe medication after diagnosing treatable injuries and illnesses.

medium security prison Prisons where some direct supervision is maintained and prisoners have recreational activities and visitation. These environments are relaxed. The level of security of each prison is determined by its physical composition and the classification of its prisoners.

mens rea The second element that must be established to prove that an accused committed a crime. It means the guilty mind the perpetrator had at the time of the commission of the crime.

minimum security prison A prison where inmates are housed that allows them freedom of activities under little supervision of correctional officers. They are typically low risk inmates. The level of security of each prison is determined by its physical composition and the classification of its prisoners.

misdemeanors A nonserious crime that carries a penalty of less than a year in jail, fine, or probation. These actions are not viewed as offenses against the state or people.

negligence tort A breach of a common law or statutory duty to act reasonably towards those who may foreseeable be harmed by ones conduct.

no bill A grand jury returns a no bill when it does not return a true bill after finding that probable cause exists to justify a case to go to trial. Because there is no showing of probable cause, the suspect is released and freed.

nominal damages Given in cases that actually show no real damage. These are damages that may be awarded when it can be shown that a technical violation occurred.

parole A status attained by incarcerated prisoners who serve most of their sentence in prison before being granted release into the free community. They serve the remainder of their sentence in the community under restrictive conditions and the supervision of a parole officer.

parole board A body of people either appointed by the governor or elected to determine if incarcerated offenders should be granted early release. The disciplinary record of an inmate could affect the decision of the parole board.

pat-down search A search involving a corrections officer moving his or her hands along the outside of a prisoner's clothing in an effort to detect contraband hidden on the prisoner's body. A pat-down search does not require a same sex officer.

plaintiff A person or party who initiates an action against another person or party in a civil action seeking damages for injuries sustained.

preponderance of the evidence In civil law, this is the level of proof that is required to prevail in these kinds of action. In essence, the side with the greatest amount of evidence (51% or more) will win in these cases. Proof beyond a reasonable doubt does not apply in civil cases.

pre-sentence investigation **(PSI)** An investigation into the life of the defendant before sentence is imposed by the judge. The purpose of the investigation is to determine more about the guilty person by ascertaining information on his criminal history, education, family life, and employment record. This allows probation officers to make recommendations and judges to make informed decisions before imposing a sentence.

Prison Litigation Reform Act of 1995 A federal law limiting federal judges' power to order remedies for right violations in corrections institutions and imposing additional requirements for prisoners seeking to file civil rights lawsuits.

prisoners' rights movement A period that started in the 1960s and continued into the latter 1980s. During this period, the Supreme Court and many federal courts acknowledged that prisoners had constitutional rights that went ignored prior to the 1960s. The movement gave inmates constitutional entitlements and guarantees to the First, Fifth, Eighth, and Fourteenth Amendments. The courts also provided prisoners with a host of remedies to have their complaints heard. Prior to the prisoners' rights movement, prisoners were considered to be "slaves" of the state without standings to have their complaints heard before the courts. The period of the movement is often referred to as the period of judicial activism.

prisoners' rights revolution See prisoners' rights movement.

prisons for profit Refers to prisons that are privately owned corporations and operated independently of state control. In contemporary society, these prisons are growing because of their appeal to save tax dollars.

privatization The process by which private individuals and corporations become involved in the management and operations of correctional institutions. Privatization refers to private prisons.

probable cause The level of belief needed to lead a reasonable person to believe that a particular person committed a particular crime. The level of proof needed by law enforcement officers to obtain a search and/or an arrest warrant.

probation A legal status from a court which allows a sentence to be served within the community under restrictive conditions and the supervision of a probation officer. During probation, a sentence of incarceration is suspended, but the person may be imprisoned for violating probation conditions or committing a new crime.

procedural law Rules that specify how statutes should be applied against those who violate the law.

public order mandate The governmental task of maintaining law and order and protecting society from crime and the criminal elements. This mandate sometimes runs counter to the preservation of individual rights and civil liberties. Police and others in law enforcement are charged with having to balance both concerns.

punitive damages Designed to punish prison officials (defendants) for severely bad conduct.
This occurs if the defendant has engaged in reckless or willful negligence.

qualified immunity Limited protection against civil lawsuits enjoyed by government officials for decisions made and actions taken within the scope of their authority and law.

reasonable doubt The legal level of doubt that is required to find a defendant not guilty of having committed a crime and to acquit him or her of the charges alleged.

reasonable expectation of privacy The concept that usually provides the basis for Fourth Amendment decisions on the permissibility of searches. In prison settings, the courts have tended to regard it as unreasonable for prisoners to expect that their clothing and cells will receive protection from searches. However, this concept applies to people in the free community and protects them from unlawful intrusion.

reasonable suspicion The legal level of belief that requires police officers to stop and frisk suspects.

recidivism When an offender who had been released from confinement engages in more crime or violate a condition of release and is subsequently returned to prison. It is estimated that near 60 percent of all offenders recidivate.

regulation Legal rules created by government agencies, including state departments of corrections.

rehabilitation Treatment programs designed to reform offenders so that they can be successfully reintegrated back into society. Programs intended to rehabilitate offenders provide them with educational, individual and group counseling, job training, and coping skills.

restitution Punishment that requires the offender to repay the victim with compensation or an area of community service that is equivalent to the harm done.

retribution Punitive punishment or punishment for the sake of punishment. This occurs when offenders get their just deserts for the crime that they have committed.

RNA Single-strand molecules of a type of nucleic acid. RNA is the abbreviation of ribonucleic acid.

Section 1983 Federal statute used by prisoners to file lawsuits against state prison officials alleging that those officials violated the prisoner' constitutional rights. This type of remedy is considered the favorite among prisoners who challenge constitutional violations and conditions of confinement.

secure confinement These are traditional places of imprisonment where security and custody are obvious. Inmates or prisoners are constantly watched and are deprived of freedom of movement because they are in cells.

separation of powers The doctrine that power is divided among three branches of government: the legislature, judicial, and the executive. Each branch has a different function: to make the law, to interpret the law, and to execute the law. The purpose of separating power was to create a balance of power so that no one agency would have complete control of all three governmental functions.

social control The process by which people confirm their behaviors to standards required by law. It can be seen as the organized way that society respond to behavior that it considers troubling, threatening, or bothersome. It can be seen as punishment, segregation, or isolating for committing behaviors that are repugnant to the law or rules that regulate aspects of social life.

special master An outsider, often a lawyer, law professor, or retired correctional official, appointed by a federal judge to oversee either the details of the litigation and negotiation process or the details of implementing the remedies for constitutional violations. Special masters are usually lawyers appointed by the court to oversee that changes are made to correctional facilities such as traditional prisons and jails.

State Constitutional Rights Act Legal rights given to prisoners by each states.

statutes The law created by the people's elected representatives in legislatures. Statutes are subjected to changes as standards of decency evolve. They can vary from state to state.

stop and frisk A procedure that was created at the case of Terry v. Ohio. It allows police officers to stop and pat down suspects for protection purposes. Stop and frisks are justified when police officers have reasonable suspicion that a potential offender is about to engage in criminal behavior.

strict liability tort Liability that does not depend on actual negligence or intent to harm. It is premised on the breach of an absolute duty to make something safe.

strip search A search requiring prisoners to remove their clothing and submit to visual examination of their entire body if reasonable suspicion exists to believe that a prisoner, visitor, or employee is trying to smuggle contraband into the facility.

substantive law The body of law that defines the rights and obligations of each person in society.

term of court The period that the Supreme Court is in session. In the United States, the Supreme Courts starts to hear and decide cases in October and continues until June. Despite its ability to agree to hear a case, the Court reserves the right not to rule in a case if it chooses.

tort A civil wrong, typically pursued via a lawsuit seeking monetary recovery for injury caused by another person or corporation. A violation of a duty imposed by law or the existence of a legal duty to plaintiff, breach of that duty leads to damages as a result of the breach. Civil liberty lawsuits under tort law help to raise jail officials' awareness and motivation to act regarding inmates' safety within the jail.

tort law The field of law that provides the basis of civil lawsuits seeking damages for personal injuries or property damages.

trail de nova A new trail on the entire case on both questions of fact and issues of law. Another is held as if the first or original trail never occurred.

true bill Indictment returned by the grand jury which essentially gives prosecutors permission to take the matter to trial.

U.S. Circuit Court of Appeals The intermediate appellate courts in the federal system that handle initial appeals on cases within a specific geographical region. In the U.S., there are 13 Circuit Courts of Appeal that have jurisdiction to review cases arising in the US and its territories.

U.S. District Court The trial courts in the federal courts system. There are approximately 94 such courts. The jurisdiction of each court includes several states.

U.S. Supreme Court The court of the last resort. It is the most powerful court in the United States. It has both original and appellate jurisdiction. Its decisions are biding on all jurisdictions in the U.S. and therefore many of its decision serve to influence public policy. It is made up of one chief justice and eight associate justices all given lifetime appointments. It is the only court that is constitutionally mandated.

venue A jurisdiction over which a judge exercises authority to act in an official capacity. A place where a trial is held.

writ of certiorari An order of a superior court requesting that the records of an inferior court be brought forward for review or inspection. A legal protection used to ask the U.S. Supreme Court to accept a case for hearing by calling up the case from a lower court. This writ is granted as a matter of discretion.

writ of error A legal document issued by an appellate court for the purpose of correcting an error revealed in the record of a lower court proceeding.

writ of mandamus An order of a superior court commanding that a lower court, administrative body, or executive body perform a specific function.

INDEX

ABOUT THE AUTHORS

James F. Anderson is an Associate Professor of Criminal Justice at the University of Missouri at Kansas City in the Department of Sociology, Criminal Justice, and Criminology. He attended the George J. Beto College of Criminal Justice at Sam Houston State University where he was awarded the Ph.D. in Criminal Justice. He received a Master of Science in Criminology from Alabama State University. He has published over twenty-five articles and a text in the area of criminal justice. He is currently writing a text on criminological theory.

Laronistine Dyson is Director of Admissions and Recruitment at Mississippi Valley State University. She received the Master of Arts degree in Interpersonal and Public Communication from Bowling Green State University. She has published over twenty scholarly articles in the areas of boot camps; crime and public health care; jail suicides; correctional managers leadership styles; police liability; psychology and others. She has co-authored a book entitled Boot Camps: An Intermediate Sanction. She has recently completed a consulting project on ethics for the Kentucky State Police and is currently co-authoring a text on community policing.